LIVERPOOL

LIVERPOOL

THE STORY OF A FOOTBALL CLUB IN 101 LIVES

ANTON RIPPON

WHITE OWL

AN IMPRINT OF PEN & SWORD BOOKS LTD.
YORKSHIRE - PHILADELPHIA

First published in Great Britain in 2020 by
PEN AND SWORD WHITE OWL
An imprint of
Pen & Sword Books Ltd
Yorkshire - Philadelphia

ISBN 978 1 52676 778 3

Typeset in Times New Roman 11.5/14 by
SJmagic DESIGN SERVICES, India.
Printed and bound in the UK by TJ Books Limited.

Pen & Sword Books Ltd incorporates the Imprints of Pen & Sword Books
Archaeology, Atlas, Aviation, Battleground, Discovery, Family History, History,
Maritime, Military, Naval, Politics, Railways, Select, Transport, True Crime,
Fiction, Frontline Books, Leo Cooper, Praetorian Press, Seaforth Publishing,
Wharncliffe and White Owl.

For a complete list of Pen & Sword titles please contact
PEN & SWORD BOOKS LIMITED
47 Church Street, Barnsley, South Yorkshire, S70 2AS, England
E-mail: enquiries@pen-and-sword.co.uk
Website: www.pen-and-sword.co.uk

Or
PEN AND SWORD BOOKS
1950 Lawrence Rd, Havertown, PA 19083, USA
E-mail: Uspen-and-sword@casematepublishers.com
Website: www.penandswordbooks.com

Contents

Contents

Introduction

'To say that these men paid their shillings to watch twenty-two hirelings kick a ball is merely to say that a violin is wood and catgut, that Hamlet is so much paper and ink.' So wrote J. B. Priestley in *The Good Companions* in 1929. It is my favourite literary passage.

Ninety-odd years later, football has changed so much. Whereas for Priestley's fan 'it offered you more than a shilling's worth of material for talk during the rest of the week', now you almost need a bank loan to pay for a season ticket to watch Premier League football. Or you can stop at home and watch Sky Sports, although that is hardly the same thing.

And yet football has also stayed the same. Football clubs are not simply businesses. They go far beyond that, filling a unique gap in the emotional lives of hundreds of thousands of people. As Priestley put it, 'cheering together, thumping one another on the shoulders, swapping judgements like lords of the earth', they have pushed their way through a turnstile 'into another and altogether more splendid kind of life'.

And it is other people's lives that have made these clubs. Players, managers, directors – down the decades, across more than a century, Liverpool Football Club has been moulded by men whose talents have been revered (and sometimes jeered), management skills applauded (and sometimes criticised), and ownership motives occasionally questioned, because supporters care more than anyone who is not a fan can imagine.

In this book, I have attempted to tell the story of this great football club through the lives of 101 people, players and managers. It does not pretend to be a list of all the best players because that is too subjective, although you will probably find most of your favourites here. It is a collection of men whose stories mirror the story of Liverpool.

So here we go. I wonder what John Houlding would have made of Jürgen Klopp?

John Houlding

What do you do when you find yourself with a football ground but no football club? In 1892, self-made Liverpool businessman John Houlding – his father was a cowkeeper – faced such a dilemma. Everton, the club that he had helped prosper were unhappy with the man who was now their landlord. So, they had decided to move. It was a financial blow for Houlding. There would now be no rent for the ground coming in, and on match days supporters would no longer visit the public houses that he owned around the ground to drink the Beacon Ales produced by his brewery in Tynemouth Street in the Everton district of Liverpool.

Houlding did the obvious thing – he started another club. Everton left Anfield – already 'the most popular [football ground] in the country' according to the *Liverpool Mercury* – and went off to the north side of Stanley Park, to what would become known as Goodison Park. Houlding was not allowed to retain the Everton name and so Anfield became the home of the 'Liverpool Association Football Club'.

On Thursday, 1 September 1892, the inaugural match at Goodison – a friendly between First Division rivals Everton and Bolton Wanderers – took place before a crowd of 10,000. On the same day, at Anfield Road, the *Liverpool Mercury* reported that 'before a moderate attendance, Councillor John Houlding kicked-off' Liverpool's first ever match, which was a friendly against Rotherham Town, champions of the Midland League. In the final minute 'the visitors got well up and scored their first goal, retiring, beaten by 7 goals to 1.' Scotsman Malcolm McVean, a signing from Third Lanark, scored Liverpool's first ever goal and Scotland international Tom Wyllie, who had joined Liverpool from Everton, scored a hat-trick. Two days later, Liverpool, beat Higher Walton 8-0 in their first match in the Lancashire League, although the attendance was again in the low hundreds.

Houlding's pubs would soon be full again on match days. However, as his new club grew apace, he, too, would move on. In 1897, he was elected Lord Mayor of Liverpool – he represented the Everton ward for the Conservatives – and he held office in other public organisations as well as the Freemasons and the Orange Order.

The spat that had turned into a full-scale disagreement, and which resulted in the birth of Liverpool FC, had begun when Houlding increased the interest on the money he had put into Everton. Then he purchased from John Orrell, a fellow brewer, the land on which the Anfield ground stood. Orrell still owned land adjacent to Anfield – where stands had been erected, crowds of 8,000 watched Everton in the Football League, and an England v Ireland international was staged in 1889. Houlding wanted Everton to raise capital to buy both his land – which would have returned him a large profit – and Orrell's. The row had festered for a long time, not least because Everton's dressing room was on licensed premises, namely the Sandon Hotel, which Houlding happened to own. In March 1892, an extraordinary general meeting of the Everton club removed Houlding, the club's president, and his loyalists Tom Howarth and Alex Nisbet from the executive. So, it was that disaffected Everton members upped sticks, Liverpool FC was born and with it one of the greatest rivalries in football.

As Houlding faded from the scene, William Barclay, who was previously with Everton, became Liverpool's first secretary (in reality secretary-manager). An application to join the Football League's newly formed Second Division was turned down so Liverpool joined the Lancashire League and in front of home crowds of 3,000 to 4,000 won the title on goal average from Blackpool. In September 1893, thieves broke into the shop of pawnbroker and furniture dealer Charles Gibson in Derby Buildings and stole the Lancashire League and Liverpool and District Cup trophies that were displayed there. It cost Liverpool – or rather Houlding – £127 to replace them.

John Houlding died on 17 March 1902 in Cimiez, Nice. He was in his 69th year and had been ill for some time. A year earlier, Liverpool FC had been crowned First Division champions.

John McKenna

In July 1920, the *Liverpool Echo* commented that 'for capability and harmony Liverpool's board show a fine example. The Liverpool shareholders admire the fact that the fraternal spirit of Mr John McKenna, the leading authority on football in these parts, in sitting on the board under the chairmanship of Mr Williams.' One year later *Athletic News* reported that:

> Mr John McKenna, president of the Football League, has resigned from the board of directors of Liverpool Football Club in protest against the action of the shareholders in not re-electing Messrs McQueen and Keating …. Mr McKenna states that he has nothing against the gentlemen elected but that he would not be a party to throwing off two men who had worked hard for the club after a successful season.

Matt McQueen was a former Liverpool player who would return as manager in February 1923. John Keating had been a director for several years. So, the fraternal spirit of which the newspaper spoke was not always evident.

John McKenna had been associated with Liverpool from the start. An Irishman, born in County Monaghan in 1855, he moved to Liverpool as a small boy and worked his way up to become a successful businessman. His first connection with football was in 1885 when he was elected chairman of a club formed by a local regiment, the 4th Lancashire Artillery Volunteers, that had been raised by a Liverpool ship owner.

John Houlding, a fellow freemason, involved McKenna in Everton, and after the split, McKenna remained with Houlding at Anfield, now the home of Liverpool. While he never held the title of manager, working alongside William Barclay, McKenna was heavily involved in recruiting the Liverpool team – mostly Scots – that won the Lancashire League in 1892-93 and took the club into the recently formed Second Division for 1893-94. One account read:

> The receipts did not repay the guarantee given to Rotherham, the first club Liverpool ever played … . The bank balance was scarcely more than a first-class professional's salary … yet Mr McKenna … got together a combination that simply scintillated with celebrities … in all thirteen professionals and sixteen reserves.

In their first season in the Football League, Liverpool won promotion to the top flight and the influence of John McKenna in that cannot be overestimated. Perhaps his biggest contribution to Liverpool, though, was to bring in Tom Watson as manager in 1896. Watson had guided Sunderland to 3 Football League championships in 4 seasons. McKenna, meanwhile, himself became one of the best-known names in football. Liverpool's chairman from 1906 to 1915 and from 1917 to 1919, he was one of the game's great administrators. In 1902, he was elected to the management committee of the Football League, became its vice-president in 1908 and president in 1910. In 1928, he was elected vice-president of the Football Association.

A contemporary writer said, 'It is rather as an organiser and a worker that he has made his mark in the game, though it would be idle to infer that he was not as good a judge of the game as most.'

'Honest' John McKenna held the office of Football League president until his death, at Walton Hospital in Liverpool on 22 March 1936. He was 82. Columnist 'Bee' of the *Liverpool Echo*, wrote:

> Mr McKenna was no respecter of persons … I have spent many afternoons at his house, chatting on football matters. He with his gout-foot lolling upon a 'humpty', the telephone at his side, a cigar box handy, a golden holder, which he prized more than any other present, and 'Ma' bringing in tea for two … . Whatever his physical disability his brain was active and sure to the end. He never forgot a date or a name. He had no fumbling for facts. From the chin to the top of his head he was as alive as any youth. I mourn a great man and a great friend.

Tom Watson

The first few years of Liverpool's existence were up and down – the Second Division title, followed by immediate relegation and then another promotion just as quickly. Stability was needed. In August 1896, Tom Watson, the manager who had taken Sunderland to 3 League titles with his 'Team of all the Talents' – he took on the Sunderland job in 1889 for 35 shillings a week and accommodation – was prised away from Newcastle Road with the promise of a better paid job at Anfield.

The *Liverpool Echo* was optimistic:

> With Tom Watson to run the show at Anfield, things should go swimmingly. The new secretary should be allowed as free a hand as possible and not be hampered in his work so long as he goes all right. It should be remembered that too many cooks spoil the broth, and it would be a pity if the Liverpool soup gets spoiled for lack of foresight ... . The team is in excellent condition ... and if they have kept the form they were in at the close of last season they will be all right for this.

Watson would see Liverpool finally established in the top flight. They finished fifth in 1896-97, 2 seasons later they were runners-up and went as far as the semi-finals of the FA Cup, and in 1900-01 won the League championship. In his 19 years in charge of Liverpool's team, he took them to another League championship, in 1905-06, and to their first FA Cup final, in 1914. The list of fine players that joined the club during Watson's tenure is impressive, starting with Alex Raisbeck, 1 of Scotland's finest centre-halves who, to be fair, had first been identified as a Liverpool target by John McKenna. Winger Arthur Goddard made over 400 appearances for Liverpool after signing for Watson, who also brought in 3 of the greatest goalkeepers the game has ever seen – Ted Doig, Elisha Scott and Sam Hardy – and Jack Parkinson and Sam Raybould who between them scored 255 goals for Liverpool. In February 1912, he signed Billy Lacey and Tom Gracie from Everton for £300 and Harold Uren who went to Goodison. Lacey would make 257 appearances for Liverpool, Gracie 33. Uren made only 24 appearances for Everton. Overall it was good business for Liverpool.

Watson, who was born in Newcastle in April 1859, started his football career with amateur clubs in his home city before taking over the administration of Newcastle East End and then Newcastle West End, the clubs that would form Newcastle United, before taking Sunderland into the Football League and those 3 top-flight titles. His success at Liverpool meant that he was the first manager to win the First Division title with 2 different clubs, a feat that Kenny Dalglish would emulate decades later.

There were also difficult times. In 1903-04 Liverpool were relegated, but they won their place straight back and then lifted the League championship again, making them the first club to win the Second and First Division titles in successive seasons.

In the years leading up to the First World War, after finishing runners-up again in 1909-10 – they finished 5 points behind champions Aston Villa – Liverpool never touched such heights again. In fact, in 1911-12 they narrowly avoided relegation, finishing only 1 point ahead of Preston North End who went down with Bury. Only wins in their last 2 matches of the season, at home to Sheffield United and away to Oldham Athletic, saved Liverpool. The 1914 FA Cup final provided a bright spot at a bleak time, although Liverpool lost to Burnley at Crystal Palace, and the Football League closed down at the end of the 1914-15 season, after which Liverpool played in wartime regional competitions until 1919.

Tom Watson would not live to see it. On 6 May 1915, aged only 56, he died from pleurisy and pneumonia. In the *Liverpool Echo*, Bee wrote, 'Poor owd Tom … I should say that he had signed more cheap and good players than any secretary in the world.'

Billy Dunlop

Billy Dunlop's career with Liverpool started slowly. The left-back who arrived at Anfield in January 1895 via Kilmarnock and the Paisley club, Abercorn, cost £35. He was 20 and Liverpool used him sparingly at first. In his first season, he made only 4 appearances in the First Division, his debut coming on a rain-soaked Monday afternoon at Anfield in March 1895 when a 3-2 defeat to Sunderland pretty much sealed Liverpool's fate. Dunlop was in the team that lost the 'test match' to Bury at neutral Ewood Park which saw them relegated. He played 12 times when Liverpool won promotion the following season, and managed only 5 games in 1896-97. It was not until his fourth season at Anfield that he won a regular place, and after that he hardly looked back.

For the next 10 years he was 1 of the first names on the team sheet each week. When Liverpool won the Football League championship in 1900-01, Dunlop missed only 2 matches, and when they repeated the feat in 1905-06 he was absent only 7 times, all through injury. That season he was capped by Scotland, in a Home International Championship match against England at Hampden Park, where the Scots won 2-1.

In September 1899, 'Abaris' writing in *The Lancashire Evening Post*, said:

> There were but few playing days in last season when Liverpool were anything worse than the best team in England ... . Circumstances, therefore, were especially favourable to William Dunlop in his making the great display that he did during the season ... a modest, unassuming young fellow, he set no store by his work, at a time when all in the football world was filled with the sound of his praises [he] argued that he was no better than in previous seasons, only shining with the team. In that he was undoubtedly wrong ... Dunlop was a very material factor

in what was the side's greatness ... . Strongly, athletically built, he has speed, strength and agility well combined, and possessing a cool head, a good eye and judgement unsusceptible to excitement.

In May 1909, his brother, John, a 20-year-old full-back, signed for Liverpool from Hurlford FC. *Athletic News* felt that should he equal the feats of his elder brother, 'who has been such a zealous servant for the Anfielders for many years' then 'J. Dunlop will be a very useful footballer for Liverpool.' Alas, John Dunlop did not make a senior appearance for them.

A year later *Athletic News* was wondering 'if we have seen the last of the dashing [Billy] Dunlop of Liverpool.' It went on: 'He did not play in the first team last season, but I notice that he is retained by Liverpool. Dunlop knew how to cover his goal, and he could use his head in every sense. The game is the poorer.'

In May 1911 Billy Dunlop announced his retirement from playing. He had made 358 appearances and scored 2 goals for Liverpool. He was then in his mid-30s and in July that year joined the Sunderland staff, working at Roker Park as a coach and a trainer for the next 30 years. The *Liverpool Echo* commented:

> There is no better known or more popular footballer in the Mersey city than William Dunlop, against whom no black mark was ever placed, and whose services at full-back were wholehearted and covered a period of sixteen years with Liverpool Football Club. Dunlop has grown grey in the service of football and one is glad to learn today that he has been appointed assistant trainer of the Sunderland club, for it means that the Scottish international obtains a good berth and retains an active hold upon the game. His host of friends will congratulate him upon his new sphere of usefulness.

During the First World War, Dunlop had worked as a masseur at the Jeffrey Hospital in Sunderland, and when war broke out again in 1939 he joined the air raid precaution casualty service. He was still working for Sunderland when he died at Stanhope, County Durham, in December 1941, aged 67.

Jack Cox

Jack Cox was 'a wily winger … who uses a fine turn of speed and centres grandly', so Liverpool were keen to retain his services when, in May 1904, he decided to sign for Fulham. Cox was Liverpool born and Liverpool had just been relegated to the Second Division of the Football League while Fulham were in the Southern League. Cox explained that he wanted to move to London to be nearer to his girlfriend but the rules tied footballers to their clubs unless there was a good reason for them to throw off the yoke. The Football League said that Cox's reasoning was insufficient and it refused to sanction the transfer. Liverpool had offered him the maximum wage, accommodation in Blackpool and a railway ticket for the season. Under those circumstances the player could not just walk away. If the club wanted to retain him, well, he was retained.

So, on 1 September 1904, instead of preparing to play for Fulham against Tottenham Hotspur at White Hart Lane, Cox lined up at outside-left against Burton United at Anfield. At the end of the season Liverpool were promoted as champions and Cox had missed only 2 games. Twelve months later he was collecting another honour, a First Division championship medal to add to the 1 he had won with Liverpool in 1900-01.

Jack Cox was born in Vauxhall Road, Liverpool, in 1877, the second of 3 children of Irish parents. His father was a bootmaker. By 1891 he was living in Blackpool with his younger brother, Bill, and their widowed mother. Jack began his football career with the South Shore Standard and South Shore clubs before signing for Second Division Blackpool in 1897. He made his debut for the Seasiders at Gainsborough Trinity in October 1897 and played in the next 16 games, scoring 12 goals. It was a remarkable strike rate for a winger, and Liverpool were 1 of several big clubs who took notice. In February 1898, Cox was transferred to Anfield for £150. It was the first 'big-money' transfer involving a Blackpool player and it went a little way to helping the Seasiders post a loss of £441 as opposed to more than £1,000 the previous season. The *Liverpool Echo* reported: 'This is a young fellow called Cox, who has been playing for the Blackpool club. He is said to be a very good outside-left wing man, 20 years of age, 11 st in weight and will be eligible to play in the next League game, when he will probably be given a trial.' In fact, Cox made his Liverpool debut at home to Notts County on 12 March 1898 and, according to *The Referee*, 'succeeded in scoring a second point for Liverpool from a corner'. The goal came late in the game and earned Liverpool a 2-0 win. He played in the next match, a 1-1 draw at home to Bolton Wanderers, but then did not reappear until the opening day of the following season in which he made 27 appearances and scored 4 goals in a campaign that saw Liverpool finish First Division runners-up to champions Aston Villa. On the final day of the season, Liverpool travelled to Villa Park knowing that a win would see them overhaul Villa, but they lost 5-0.

In March 1901, Cox won his first England cap, in a 3-0 win over Ireland at The Dell, and he won 2 more, both against Scotland. He also played in the 1902 game that was declared void after 25 people lost their lives and 500 were injured when part of a wooden terracing at Ibrox collapsed.

Jack Cox made 360 appearances for Liverpool and scored 80 goals before he returned to Blackpool on a free transfer in 1909. In 1912, aged 34, he retired from playing. Cox, who won the 100 yards footballers' race in 1902, died at Walton–on-Thames in November 1955, just short of his 78th birthday. His brother Bill, who played for Bury, Preston, Dundee and Hearts, died in 1915, of wounds suffered while serving in Dardanelles.

Sam Raybould

'A player who seems to know by intuition where the goals lie, and usually heads the goalscoring list for his club, dashing and skilful, he makes openings for himself and invariably utilises them well.' That was *The Book of Football's* 1906 assessment of Liverpool's Sam Raybould. Had Derby County seen Raybould's potential 12 years earlier, he would probably never have ended up at Anfield. The Derbyshire-born forward signed for Derby in April 1894 and on his debut scored the only goal of the game against Aston Villa, but after only 5 games for the Rams, he was allowed to rejoin Ilkeston Town for a £10 transfer fee. There were stints at Bolsover Colliery FC and Second Division New Brighton Tower before Tom Watson signed him for Liverpool in January 1900.

Raybould was 30 seconds into his second appearance for Liverpool when he scored his first goal – at Goodison Park of all places. Unfortunately, Everton recovered from that early setback to win 3-1 but the following season, 1900-01, now switched from the wing to the middle, Raybould was top scorer with 16 goals as Liverpool won the League championship for the first time. He headed the Reds' scoring list in 3 of the next 6 seasons, his 31 goals in 1902-03 making him the Football League's leading scorer. It was a Liverpool club record that stood for 30 years until Gordon Hodgson broke it.

After Raybould missed the first half of 1903-04, Liverpool were relegated along with West Bromwich Albion. His absence was not due to injury, but because the Football Association suspended him until 31 December after he become involved in an attempt by Portsmouth to sign him, together with his Liverpool club mates Billy Goldie and Jack Glover. Pompey tried to use the apparent lack of proper arrangements between the Southern League and the Football League to take them to Fratton Park but the whole affair was ruled illegal. Portsmouth were fined £100 and the players suspended for agreeing to 'financial inducements'.

Because Liverpool had offered each of the trio the maximum weekly wage for a footballer – £4 – the players could not leave on their own account. Without their star goalscorer it was Liverpool who suffered most, however. Goldie and Glover never played for the Reds again but although Raybould returned for the last 15 games, his 4 goals were not enough to save the Reds from the drop.

With Raybould in for the entire season, Liverpool bounced straight back. In the promotion season of 1904-05, when the Reds won a record 58 points, he scored 20 goals, and was on target 14 times when the League championship was won again in 1905-06. Liverpool quickly forgave him for the Portsmouth episode. In December 1905, Raybould was given the gate receipts from the First Division match against Aston Villa – there were 25,000 at Anfield that afternoon – as a benefit in recognition of his services over the previous 5 years. *Athletic News* commented, 'There are few inside-forwards superior to Raybould – a rover no longer.'

Another 17 goals in 1906-07 took his tally for Liverpool in League and FA Cup to 127 in 224 appearances before he was transferred to Sunderland in May 1907. One year later he moved to Woolwich Arsenal where he finished his top-flight career in May 1909. Raybould, who played 3 times for the Football League against the Scottish League, wound down his playing days with Chesterfield Town in the Midland League, Sutton Town and Barlborough.

In February 1910, at Chesterfield Borough Police Court, Raybould was granted a separation from his wife, Selina, on the grounds that she was a habitual drunkard. The court heard that 'after they went to live in Liverpool his wife fell in with some woman neighbours of an undesirable character and took to drink.' Life must have taken a happier turn, however as in 1939, Selina was still living with him at their house in Clowne, Derbyshire. He was working as a hewer at a colliery. Sam Raybould died in December 1953. He was 78.

Ned Doig

John Edward 'Ned' Doig was almost at the end of his career when he signed for Liverpool – for £150 from Sunderland in 1904 – but his 1 full season for the Reds was vital for the club, and he played a major part in it.

Born in Forfarshire in 1866, Doig began his career as an outside-right in Arbroath with St Helena FC before joining Arbroath in 1884. By now he had switched to keeping goal and after 2 seasons of reserve-team football made his senior debut. Three years and 2 Scotland caps later he was on his way to Blackburn Rovers. *The Blackburn Times* noted that on his debut against Notts County in November 1889, Doig 'made a very favourable impression on the spectators … his duties were light but they were smartly performed.'

After that game, however, he returned to Scotland. Then he signed for Sunderland and made his debut for the Wearsiders in a 4-0 defeat of West Bromwich Albion in September 1890. But he had not been registered for the required 7 days. The 1906 *Book of Football* reported that the Football League 'came down with a vengeance', fining Sunderland £50 and deducting 'the gallantly won points'. The League's law was 'as inexorable as the code of Medes and the Persians' but it turned out all right in the end. Ever-present in 6 of the next 14 seasons, Doig helped Sunderland win 4 League championships, and he was capped a further 4 times by Scotland.

In August 1904, after 457 appearances for the Wearsiders, his former Sunderland manager, Tom Watson, signed him for recently relegated Liverpool. The transfer was not straightforward, as reported by the *Sunderland Daily Echo and Shipping Gazette*:

> The delay, it may be mentioned, is meaning a serious loss
> to Doig, who, having been kept hanging on between the

2 clubs without being signed on by either, is drawing no pay during the period. It has been asserted that while the Sunderland club are putting no obstacles in the way of his transfer to Liverpool, they are not too eager that he should go, and most of the directors would like him to stay. And Doig himself ... is ready to stick to Sunderland, but will not himself back out of the negotiations with Liverpool unless he is forced to by a delay on the part of Liverpool. The terms that were offered him by Sunderland were generous enough, but Doig, it is said, got at loggerheads with an official, and thus the difficulty arose.

The newspaper added, 'That Mr Tom Watson, the secretary of the Liverpool AFC, is desirous of Doig's assistance is proved by the fact that he has been in repeated communication with the player, and told him to do nothing – meaning presumably not to sign for any other club – until they have settled with him.'

The business sorted, Doig made his Liverpool debut at home to Burton United on 1 September 1904, and was ever-present, playing brilliantly, as the Reds stormed away with the Second Division title. He was 37 years old, making him Liverpool's oldest debutant. That first season he kept 16 clean sheets as Liverpool conceded only 25 goals in 34 League matches. The following season, however, when Liverpool followed up with the First Division title, he played in only the first 8 matches before Sam Hardy replaced him for the remainder of the season. He made only 4 appearances in 1906-07, and 5 in 1907-08, and he was 41 years and 165 days old when he made his final appearance, at Newcastle, in April 1908, making him the oldest player to appear for the Reds. He finished his playing career with St Helens Recreationals in the Lancashire League. It is recorded that Liverpool advised him that they no longer required his services by sending him a postcard – the early 20th-century version of an email – and this sent him into a rage. He died in Liverpool in November 1919, from the effects of the so-called Spanish influenza.

Jack Parkinson

In 1899, Jack Parkinson was working as a railway clerk and living with his parents and 5 siblings in Bootle cum Linacre, where he was born in September 1883. He was scoring goals for local clubs Hertford Albion and Valkyrie when Liverpool noticed him. The Reds took him on amateur forms and then signed him as a professional in October 1903. It was the start of a Liverpool career that would last until the outbreak of the First World War and bring him 128 goals in 221 League and FA Cup appearances, together with championship medals in the First and Second Divisions, and 2 England caps. All this despite missing 6 months of the 1905-06 season after breaking a wrist against Woolwich Arsenal in the first game of the season.

His first goal for Liverpool came 15 minutes into his debut, in October 1903, against Small Heath at Muntz Street where the forerunners of Birmingham City played. When Liverpool won the Second Division title in 1904-05, Parkinson's 20 goals went a long way towards that as together with Sam Raybould and Robert Robinson he formed a prolific trio.

The following season, because of that injury, Parkinson made only 9 appearances but still scored 7 goals. It did not take him long to get back on the mark, only 5 minutes in fact when he opened the scoring in a 6-1 win over Middlesbrough at Anfield in March 1906. It was 1908-09, however, before he became a regular once more, and in 1909-10 his 30 goals made him the First Division's leading scorer. That season he scored 11 goals in his first 7 games, including a hat-trick at Nottingham Forest, 2 goals against both Manchester United and Sheffield Wednesday at Anfield and another 2 goals at Bolton, all before the end of October. When Forest visited Anfield in April 1910 they lost 7-3 and Parkinson scored 4 of Liverpool's goals that afternoon.

By then he was an England international, capped for the first time against Wales in Cardiff in March 1910. A second cap followed in April, against Scotland at Hampden Park. Over the next 3 seasons, Parkinson scored over 40 First Division goals, but the speed that had seen him win the 1905 footballers' race over 100 yards that was organised at Dundee FC (Liverpool's Jack Cox finished second, having himself won it in 1902) was deserting him, and in 1913-14 he played only 6 times in the League. Although he played in the Reds' first 2 FA Cup matches, a draw and a replay win over Barnsley, that season he did not make the final against Burnley at Crystal Palace.

His last Merseyside derby match was something to remember, though. In February 1913, he scored both goals in Liverpool's 2-0 victory at Goodison Park. In March 1914, Parkinson and Arthur Goddard were each guaranteed £350 from the receipts of the First Division match against Preston North End at Anfield.

In August 1914, now aged almost 32, Parkinson was allowed to leave Anfield and finish his playing career with Second Division Bury. He scored in each of his first 3 games for the Shakers, but played only once more and in October 1914, despite his goals, Bury released him. The *(Sheffield) Star Green 'Un* said:

> When with Liverpool, Parkinson's speed was something remarkable … in the latter days, however, he has hardly been so quick … with the result that the tolerably fast Bury wings have suffered. There is nothing so unattractive as a centre acting as a sort of tandem driver to his wing men.

Jack Parkinson went into business as a wholesale newsagent in Liverpool and when he died on 13 September 1942 at the Northern Hospital in the city, just before his 59th birthday, he was chairman of the Mersey and District Council of Wholesale and Retail Newsagents.

Note: John Parkinson of Blackpool played 1 match for Liverpool in September 1899, against Everton, and his appearance for the Reds has sometimes been credited to Jack Parkinson.

Alex Raisbeck

One wonders why with a man like A. Raisbeck on the side the Liverpool Club could ever have lost its place in the First Division of the Football League. Raisbeck is no mere first-class half-back. He is a man amongst thousands. He is fit to be ranked with the great ones of the football field, the men whose names will go down in posterity … . His great forte as a half-back is a dashing breezy versatility. He is like an intelligent automaton full wound up and warranted to last through the longest game on record … . Swift rapid movement, fierce electric rushes to him are an everlasting delight … . Of the many sons of Scotland who have crossed the border to play football, there is no one more generally admired and respected than Alec [*sic*] Raisbeck of Liverpool.

Thus, a contemporary writer in the 1905 book, *Association Football and The Men Who Made It* described the man John McKenna told Tom Watson to sign for Liverpool in May 1898.

Alex Raisbeck was only 17 when he made his debut for Hibernian after joining them from Larkhall Thistle in July 1896. Six months later, with only 10 first-team appearances for Hibs to his name, he was representing the Scottish League against the Irish League at Cliftonville. 'He is one of the youngest professionals in Scotland and certainly one of the most promising,' said *The Lancashire Evening Post*.

In March 1898, Hibs lent Raisbeck and Jack Kennedy to Stoke, who were struggling at the wrong end of the First Division. Raisbeck played in 4 League matches and 4 Test matches. Kennedy remained at Stoke for the following season but as soon as the Potters had avoided relegation, Liverpool moved in. T. T. Mac, writing in *The Scottish Referee*, said,

'Late on Saturday night I hear that Tom Watson has signed on Raisbeck for Liverpool. The Mersey Committee must have wealth galore as I understand that Raisbeck's terms are £6 weekly all year round.'

It was the beginning of a glorious career at Anfield. After Liverpool missed a League and FA Cup double in 1898-99 – the Reds were First Division runners-up and Cup semi-finalists – Raisbeck shared all the success – and the occasional stumble – for the next 10 seasons, winning 2 League championship medals and a Second Division winners' medal, and 8 caps for Scotland, 7 of them coming against England. At the age of 21 he was Liverpool's captain.

In 1915, he told the *Weekly News*:

> I liked Liverpool, so did my wife, and although the pathway had not always been strewn with roses, my time had been pleasantly spent at Anfield.... Yet I had a feeling that the sixth season [1903-04] would be my last ... at the end of the season Liverpool found itself in the unfortunate position of being relegated ... I simply could not leave my club in its day of disaster.

So, he remained to help the Reds win promotion and then another First Division title.

Before a second-round FA Cup game at Anfield in February 1909, under the headline 'The Liverpool Eleven – How Norwich Can Beat Them', an *Eastern Evening News* writer commented, 'When I saw Alex Raisbeck, the captain, there was little to draw for your readers. Raisbeck doesn't talk. He uses his head chiefly for getting the ball out of his own goalmouth. However, he is hopeful and he says the men feel "fairly easy about the result".' In fact, Liverpool lost 3-2.

Raisbeck, who was known as 'The Silent Man of Football', left Liverpool at the end of that season. In March *The Scottish Referee* had reported, 'Raisbeck seems to have completely lost his form.'

After 340 senior appearances and 21 goals for Liverpool he moved to back to Scotland with Partick Thistle before ending his playing career with Hamilton Academical where he was also manager and a director. He later managed Bristol City, Halifax Town, Chester and Bath City. Alex Raisbeck was scouting for Liverpool and living close to Anfield when he died in Walton Hospital in March 1949, aged 70.

Arthur Goddard

Almost from the start, Arthur Goddard gave Liverpool remarkable service. After Tom Watson signed him from Second Division Glossop in February 1902, he played in the last 11 games of that season, and for 9 seasons after that; out of 330 League games he missed only 25. By the time his Anfield career ended, on the eve of the First World War, Goddard had played 415 times for Liverpool and scored 80 goals, helping them to consecutive Second and First Division titles. Between 1903 and 1912 he played in 23 consecutive FA Cup ties, and he represented the Football League on 3 occasions.

From the beginning, commentators knew that Liverpool had done the right thing. On 26 February 1902, *The Lancashire Evening Post* reported:

> The directorate of the Liverpool Club, having realised their position in the League [the Reds had won the First Division title the season before but were now mid-table], and to strengthen the attack, Mr Tom Watson has just succeeded in signing-on Arthur Goddard of Glossop. Goddard learned his football in Stockport and was then transferred about 2 years ago to Glossop. He is said by excellent judges to be the finest outside-right in England. He played in the North and South match last year and this year was chosen to represent [the] English v Irish League. He is 22 years of age … . Liverpool are to be congratulated upon this important capture, for Aston Villa, Small Heath and Newcastle United, and other clubs, have all been after him.

Several other newspapers reported that 'the crack outside-right of the Glossop club' had cost 'the largest transfer fee ever known to be paid for a player' and that Glossop had been 'compelled to take this step owing to the scant support the organisation has received since Christmas.' The £460 fee could indeed have been a British record, being somewhere between the £100 that Aston Villa paid for Willie Groves in 1893 and the £700 that Andy McCombie would cost Newcastle United to sign him from Sunderland in 1904.

Goddard was born in Heaton Norris, Stockport, in 1878, which would make him 2 years older than reported at the time he joined Liverpool. Glossop paid Lancashire League Stockport County £260 for him. The Derbyshire club had just been promoted to the First Division but in Goddard's first season with them – 1899-1900 – they were relegated straight away, along with Burnley. That did not prevent *The Lancashire Evening Post* of February 1900 from saying:

> Goddard's genius should win for him a place among leading players of the game, and, combined with the gentlemanly manner characteristic of his bearing both on the field and off, ought to make him an honoured ornament of professionalism ... . Goddard has steered his course into first-class football along the extreme right, and has found the route about as rapid as are some of his bee-line bursts for goal ... he shoots from almost any position.

When Liverpool won the First Division in 1905-06, he was the only 1 of their players not to miss a game. In December 1909, he was in the side that beat Newcastle United 6-5 after being 5-2 down at half-time. His career continued at that level until 1913-14 when he lost his place in November, and he played only once more after that. He was transferred to Southern League Cardiff City, playing for them in 1914-15 before returning to Anfield to turn out for Liverpool in wartime regional league games. In September 1915, the *Liverpool Echo* reported:

> [O]n Saturday we shall revive old memories, Arthur Goddard having been chosen as outside-right. A well-preserved, gentlemanly player, with a graceful style, Goddard is able to keep time with present day football

without straining himself, and, in truth, I think his play will be all the better suited by the friendly game, because he has not to worry about trips and hacks, as in former years.

A testimonial raised enough money for Goddard to go into business on Merseyside. He was 77 when he died in Liverpool in May 1956.

Joe Hewitt

On 15 February 1908, Liverpool entertained Woolwich Arsenal at Anfield in what could loosely be called a relegation battle. True, there were still 14 matches to play, but both sides needed the points to avoid dropping further towards the bottom 2 places in the First Division. It was Liverpool who triumphed, 4-1, thanks to a hat-trick from Joe Hewitt. His first goal was a shot from 25 yards out, his second was a 'lightning shot', and his third came from close range. It was Hewitt's second hat-trick of the season. Back in November, Notts County had been hit for 6 at Anfield, and Hewitt bagged 3 of them. Five weeks after Arsenal went home empty-handed, Liverpool took a 4-0 half-time lead at home to Manchester United and ran out 7-4 winners. Hewitt scored 2 of them, the first and the last, in the 4th and 89th minute.

Joe Hewitt was born in Chester in May 1881 and was playing for Newtown Rangers in the Chester League when someone recommended that Sunderland take a closer a look at him. He played 5 times and scored once when Sunderland won the First Division title in 1901-02, and had scored 10 goals in 37 goals for the Wearsiders before Tom Watson signed him for Liverpool in February 1904, along with Sunderland's Robert Robinson following 'protracted negotiations'. Newspapers reported that 'the transfer fee has not been divulged but it is, we understand, only moderate compared to some that have lately been paid.' Later reports suggested that Hewitt had been valued at £50. The papers reported that 'each man has proved himself capable and versatile'.

In his first full season with Liverpool, Robinson was the Reds' leading scorer with 23 goals from 32 games as they won the Second Division. He scored 11 goals from 34 games when they lifted the First Division title the following season, and altogether he would score 65 goals in 271 League and FA Cup games for the Reds before being transferred to Tranmere Rovers in 1912.

Hewitt, meanwhile, played only 9 times in the successful Second Division season of 1904-05, but when Liverpool won the First Division in 1905-06, after being moved from inside-forward to centre-forward he missed only 1 game and top-scored with 23 goals.

Despite injuries and ill-health – and the form of Sam Raybould – hampering his latter days at Anfield, he remained a potent force in front of goal until the 1909-10 season when he managed only 4 appearances (but still scored twice). In May 1910, the *Cricket and Football Field* wondered, 'How would Joe Hewitt with a pair of good shooting boots on suit the Wanderers in the Second Division next season? Joe is big, robust player and is far from being done with yet.' That year, after scoring 69 goals in 164 appearances in his Liverpool career, Hewitt moved to Bolton Wanderers and marked his debut with a goal against Stockport County, but after playing in the first 11 games for the recently relegated Trotters, and scoring 3 times, he was out in the cold.

After 4 games for Southern League Reading in 1911-12, Hewitt retired from playing and returned to Anfield, where he was to work in a variety of behind-the-scenes roles until 1964 when he retired as the match-day press box attendant. Liverpool awarded him a pension. He had been living in a retirement home in Croxteth when he died in November 1971, aged 90. The *Liverpool Echo* reported, 'He was a very popular figure at Anfield throughout his sixty years there and always had an anecdote about some of the great figures in the game to keep his audience amused.'

His life had not been without drama. In March 1907, Joe Hewitt had tried to save the life of his next-door neighbour, Sarah Ann Sweeney, in Finchley Road, Anfield. Her nightdress caught fire as she got out of bed and, rather than imperil her baby who was also in the bedroom, she ran to Hewitt's house. He extinguished the flames but Mrs Sweeney died from shock. The story was told under the headline 'Footballer's Pluck'.

Sam Hardy

On 7 January 1905, Liverpool, third in the Second Division behind Bolton Wanderers and Manchester United, met fifth-placed Chesterfield at Anfield. Despite the closeness of the teams in the table, and Liverpool having to play with 10 men for a spell after Sam Raybould collided with an opponent, the home side ran out 6-1 winners. *Athletic News* reported that 'a weaker display than that given by the Chesterfield men has not been seen at Anfield this season' and that 'fully four-fifths of the play was contested in their quarter of the field.'

In goal for Chesterfield that afternoon was Sam Hardy, who signed for them by the light of a village lamp in nearby Newbold where he had been playing for the White Star club. The story goes that 20-year-old Hardy would not put pen to paper until his weekly wage had been raised from 5 shillings to 18 shillings. He could hardly have been blamed for asking for more. The maximum wage for a footballer was then £4. Hardy made his Chesterfield debut at Woolwich Arsenal in April 1903. He let in 3 goals that day but kept his place. In fact, over the next 2 seasons he was to miss only 2 games before Tom Watson signed him for Liverpool in May 1905. Watson had been impressed on that day back in January, when, but for Hardy's heroics against a relentless tide of red shirts, Liverpool would surely have got well into double figures.

Liverpool paid a £500 transfer fee for a goalkeeper that the *Derbyshire Times and Chesterfield Herald* described as having 'in judgement and resource ... few equals'. In 1905-06, Hardy came in for the ninth game of the season, replacing Ned Doig against Nottingham Forest at Anfield, and kept his place for the rest of the season. On 2 December, when Liverpool beat table-topping Aston Villa 3-0 at Anfield, Hardy saved a penalty from Billy Garraty. Thereafter, there were few stumbles as the Reds took the First Division title and reached the FA Cup semi-finals.

In 1907 Hardy was capped by England for the first time, against Ireland at Goodison Park. He won 14 full caps with Liverpool and added a further 7 after he was transferred to Aston Villa in June 1912. Liverpool had awarded him a benefit match, against Woolwich Arsenal at Anfield on Easter Monday 1911 with a guarantee of £500, but, a year later, newspapers reported that he 'had some trouble with Liverpool due to his desire to reside in Chesterfield.' He had made 239 League and FA Cup appearances while at Anfield.

Villa presumably had no such concerns about where Hardy laid his head, and he won 2 FA Cup winners' medals with them, in 1913 and 1920. During the First World War, he served in the Royal Navy and guested for Plymouth Argyle. He ended his playing career with Nottingham Forest, who paid Villa £1,000 for his services, and he helped them win promotion from the Second Division in 1921-22. An injury, sustained against Newcastle United in October 1924, forced him to retire. He was 42. After football he ran a pub, a billiard hall and a hotel. In October 1925, he was taken to hospital in Chesterfield after what several newspapers described as an attack of meningitis, although after his recovery from 'lying dangerously ill', *The Yorkshire Post* reported that he was suffering from 'a slight fracture at the base of the skull'. Whatever the problem, Sam Hardy – who was 1 of 7 children of a Derbyshire coalminer – lived until the age of 84. When he died in Chesterfield in October 1966, Ken Campbell, the goalkeeper who replaced Hardy at Anfield, told the *Liverpool Echo*'s Leslie Edwards:

> His passing is a great sorrow to me, not only because he was the finest goalkeeper of his age, but also because he was such a gentleman. When I was young and making my way in the game, he took me out time and again and gave me the benefit of his tremendous experience.

Donald McKinlay

Nineteen-year-old full-back Donald McKinlay must have enjoyed his debut for Liverpool. On 20 April 1910, he made his first appearance for the Reds in a First Division match against Nottingham Forest at Anfield. The previous season Liverpool had missed relegation by only 2 points. This time, for part of the season at least, they had an outside chance of the title. But now, even though Forest were despatched 7-3 – Jack Parkinson scoring 4 of Liverpool's goals – the Reds were still 6 points behind Aston Villa with only 2 games and, in those days, only 4 points remaining. Despite beating Villa 2-0 on the final day of the season, Liverpool had to be content with runners-up spot.

For McKinlay, though, it was a satisfactory beginning – and there would be many more games, and plenty of success to come, albeit he had a slow start, playing only 10 times in his first 3 seasons, and making only 68 League appearances before the competition closed down because of the First World War. He did, however, play in Liverpool's first FA Cup final, the 1914 defeat at the hands of Burnley.

McKinlay had begun his playing career with Glasgow junior clubs Newton Swifts, Rutherglen Woodburn and Newton Villa before signing for Liverpool in January 1910. For a defender, he was not a tall man, standing only 5ft 8ins, but he weighed in at a solid 11st 5lbs. He was no pure defender, however. In a Liverpool career that spanned 20 years and 433 League and FA Cup appearances, he scored 33 goals for the Reds because, apart from playing at full-back and centre-half, he also appeared in the forward line.

After League football resumed in 1919, McKinlay's career went from strength to strength. He skippered Liverpool to successive League championship-winning seasons, in 1921-22 and 1922-23, and he was ever-present in the latter. In February 1922, at the age of 30, he won his first Scotland cap, against Wales at Wrexham, where the Scots lost on a heavy snow-covered pitch described by the *Wrexham Leader* as like 'a Christmas pudding covered in white sauce'. The following month he was capped again, against Northern Ireland at Parkhead where Scotland won 2-1. He was dropped for the England game at Villa Park, where the Scots retained the British Home Championship.

On another snow-covered pitch, at Upton Park in January 1926, McKinlay scored perhaps the most remarkable goal of his career when his 15th-minute shot from the halfway line was totally misjudged by West Ham goalkeeper Alex Kane, who had just joined from Portsmouth. It gave Liverpool the lead and they went on to win 2-1.

In September 1928, in the second match of the season, at Villa Park, McKinlay tore muscles in his right calf. It left Liverpool with 10 men for the whole of the second half and they went down 3-1. The *Sheffield Daily Telegraph* reported that 'it is feared that he [McKinlay] may not play again this season, which is to be the occasion of his third benefit.' Indeed, McKinlay did not play again for Liverpool. The injury signalled the end of his first-class career. However, on 6 May 1929, *The Staffordshire Sentinel* reported, 'After the Liverpool-Manchester City match, McKinlay, who has finished his career with Liverpool after 20 years' service, received a cheque for £468, his fourth benefit.'

At the age of 38, he signed for Lancashire Combination club Prescot Combination. In March 1930, *The Lancashire Evening Post* reported that 'McKinlay was a sound defender for the visitors' who, however, lost 3-1 to Darwen at the Anchor ground.

After leaving football in 1931, McKinlay was mine host at several hostelries in the Liverpool area. In September 1959, he was admitted to Broadgreen Hospital in the city, and died a few days later, aged 69. Writing in the *Liverpool Echo*, Leslie Edwards said, 'To his colleagues at Anfield he was the typically quiet Scot, as sound and solid physically as he was mentally. I remember him with close-cropped iron-grey hair. His driving of a dead-ball was phenomenal.'

Eph Longworth

On 14 May 1910, the *Cricket and Football Field* reported on Liverpool's new signings. Of 22-year-old Ephraim Longworth, the Saturday evening publication said, 'He is young, nicely built (11st 7lbs) and able. Surely from their 7 full-backs Liverpool will be able to scrape together a really first-class pair?'

Born in Halliwell, Lancashire, on 2 October 1887, the fifth of 6 children of a cotton spinner, Longworth was working as a cotton piercer in a local mill and playing amateur football with clubs such as Chorley Road Congregationals, Bolton St Luke's and Halliwell Rovers before turning professional with Hyde St George. In June 1907, Bolton Wanderers took him on but, a year later, and without having appeared in the Trotters' first team, he moved to London to play for Leyton FC (not to be confused with Clapton/Leyton Orient as has often been reported) in the Southern League. The *Athletic News* of 17 August 1908 said, 'Longworth comes from Bolton with a good reputation.'

It was from Leyton that Tom Watson signed Longworth, who stood 5ft 8½ins tall, at the end of a season in which Liverpool had finished First Division runners-up and Tom Chorlton had been ever-present at right-back. Chorlton began 1910-11 as first choice, too, but after a handful of games he lost his place to the newcomer Longworth. After that Chorlton, who had made 122 senior appearances for Liverpool, never appeared in the Reds' first team again, and in 1912 he was transferred to Manchester United for whom he played only 4 times before dropping into non-League football with Stalybridge Celtic. In contrast, Longworth was hardly missing from Liverpool's senior side after that. By the time he retired in 1928, he had made 370 League and FA Cup appearances, captained his club and country, and won consecutive Football League championship medals, in 1921-22 and 1922-23, and an FA Cup runners-up medal in 1914. In those days players did not wear numbers on their shirts but Longworth was always instantly recognisable thanks to the lock of hair that fell over his forehead.

His final game came towards the end of 1927-28 and it was his only appearance that season. On 21 April, he played against Birmingham at St Andrew's. Liverpool, struggling with injuries, were forced to recall the man who had once been the first name on the team sheet week after week. Longworth played at left-back, with Bert Shears at right-back. Shears, too, had been recalled to help deal with the defensive emergency. Both clubs were in the bottom half of the First Division and needed the points. Birmingham won 3-2 and Eph Longworth's playing career ended that day.

What a magnificent career it had been, and how many more games he would have added, had it not been for losing 4 seasons to the First World War, when he played in 2 Victory internationals, precursors to the 5 England caps that he would win, starting with the 5-4 victory over Scotland at Hillsborough in April 1920. That year, along with Liverpool teammate Jack Bamber, he also toured South Africa with a Football Association representative party. In one of the early matches of that tour, Longworth's nose was broken, but, according to the *Liverpool Echo*, he returned to Anfield 'with a budget of new ideas and suggestions and comments'.

In his second full international he captained England against Belgium in Brussels in May 1921. He was 35 when he won his last cap, in the 2-2 draw at Hampden Park in April 1923. That was a supreme example of the fact Longworth held off the challenge of younger players for so long. He was no pure defender, either, and always looked to set his attackers on their way with a carefully placed pass, rather than simply booting the ball upfield to clear his lines. He rarely ventured forward himself, though, and, despite those 370 appearances, he never scored a goal for Liverpool. After retiring he joined the coaching staff at Anfield. Ephraim Longworth died in Liverpool on 7 January 1968, aged 80.

Billy Lacey

In February 1912, Liverpool manager Tom Watson did a smart piece of business. He signed Billy Lacey and Tom Gracie from Everton in a deal that took Liverpool's Harold Uren and £300 to Goodison Park in return. While Uren made only 24 appearances for Everton before being transferred to Wrexham in 1913, Gracie, who had played 13 times for Everton, added 33 Liverpool games to his tally before returning to his native Scotland to play for Hearts, for a £400 transfer fee. Alas, in October 1915 he would die from leukaemia.

Lacey, meanwhile, would remain at Anfield until 1924, by which time, despite the interruption of the First World War, he had made 257 appearances, scored 29 goals, and won 2 Football League championship medals. In 1923, the *Liverpool Echo* wondered whether there was ever a transfer that was so valuable to Liverpool.

Lacey was an Irishman, born in County Wexford in 1889. He played for the Dublin club Shelbourne before Everton signed him in August 1908. A versatile footballer who could play in several positions, he scored 11 goals in 40 games for Everton before making the short journey to Anfield, where he made his biggest impression on the wing, although he managed only 1 goal in each of the First Division title-winning seasons, despite being a regular at outside-right. When it came to finding the back of the net, the FA Cup seemed more to his liking and when Liverpool reached the Cup final in 1914, Lacey scored 5 goals in 8 games. Barnsley had particular reason to remember him. In the first-round tie that ended 1-1 at Anfield it was his goal that earned Liverpool another chance, and he scored a last-minute winner in the Thursday afternoon replay at Oakwell, although it was the Reds' goalkeeper, Ken Campbell, who was judged to be the game's real hero with a fine second-half display to keep Barnsley at bay.

After the Football League was suspended in 1915, Lacey returned to Ireland to guest for Belfast United and Linfield, but when the competition resumed in 1919 he was back at Anfield. His international career had begun in 1909, when there was only 1 'Ireland' team, but after the political upheaval that gave birth to the Irish Free State, he was capped by both North and South, as, indeed, were many players. Altogether he won 23 caps and captained Ireland when they won the British Home Championship in 1914. His 2 goals at Ayresome Park in February that year helped the Irish to their first victory in England, when they won 3-0. In goal for England that afternoon was Lacey's former Liverpool teammate, Sam Hardy.

His last appearance for Liverpool was on 12 March 1924, at Burnden Park, after which he moved across the Mersey to join Third Division North club New Brighton. He was the first Rakers player to be capped but the honour was soured when, against England at Goodison Park, he injured a knee, which resulted in New Brighton claiming £200 damages from the Irish FA. After undergoing a cartilage operation in March 1925, Lacey did not play for the Rakers again. He had managed only 7 games for them before moving back to his first club, Shelbourne. On 11 May 1930, more than 21 years since his international debut, Lacey played at right-back when Ireland beat Belgium 3-1 in Brussels. At 40 years and 255 days old, it makes him the oldest player ever to be capped by the Republic of Ireland. He later managed the Bohemians club – with whom he won the League of Ireland championship and Shield, and the FAI Cup – and also coached the Irish Free State national team. In April 1936, the *Liverpool Echo* reported, 'Soccer football has slumped badly in the Irish Free State this season, the standard being very low. Yet Smiler Billy Lacey had had a successful time again.'

Billy Lacey died in May 1969, aged 79, in Broadgreen Hospital, Liverpool. A widower with 1 son, he had recently been living in Basil Grange care home in Sandfield Park.

Elisha Scott

Writing in the *Belfast Telegraph* on 20 January 1913, 'Ralph the Rover' said, 'I have been informed that Liverpool have been asked by several important League clubs in England to part with Elisha Scott. They do not intend to do so, although an offer they received was of a high order.'

Two weeks earlier, 'Impartial' of *The Northern Whig*, said:

> On the subject of possible internationals, an eye must be kept upon young Elisha Scott, who went from Broadway United, Belfast, to play for Liverpool in the English League against Newcastle United on New Year's Day, and to whose exhibition of goalkeeping against the classic Tyneside forwards the English critics gave unstinted praise. Elisha is a younger brother of the great William, which proves that goalkeeping, like wooden legs, sometimes runs in families.

Elisha Scott, brother of Billy Scott, the Irish international goalkeeper who had recently moved from Everton to Leeds City, had indeed enjoyed a magnificent debut for Liverpool at St James's Park on the first day of the year. And Liverpool had received several offers – including 1 from Newcastle themselves. Elisha might have moved to Tyneside had not Liverpool manager Tom Watson talked him out of it. The Magpies were prepared to pay £1,000 for the goalkeeper who had denied them, and Scott felt it was a good move because he could see no chance of dislodging Liverpool's regular keeper, Ken Campbell. But Watson was adamant that the 19-year-old's future lay at Anfield, although even the Liverpool manager could not have imagined just what lay ahead. Scott would remain at Anfield for 21 years, making 467 League and FA Cup appearances, winning 2 League championship medals and 31 caps for Ireland when international football in Britain was pretty much restricted to the British Home Championship and there was no World Cup, European Championships and few friendly matches to help stack up a large number of caps. He was 41 when he made his final international appearance. Not bad for a goalkeeper who stood only 5ft 9ins tall. His number of Liverpool appearances would have easily passed 500 had he, like his contemporaries, not missed 4 seasons when the Football League closed down during the First World War.

Elisha Scott anecdotes decorate the story of Liverpool Football Club, such as the one that has him making an astounding save against Blackburn Rovers at Anfield (some versions put the game at Ewood Park) and a supporter racing on to kiss him.

When Liverpool won the First Division in consecutive seasons, 1921-23, Scott missed only 3 games out of 84. By December 1928, however, now in his mid-30s, he lost his place to the South African Arthur Riley. The *Sheffield Independent* reported that:

> Riley's inclusion in the Liverpool team has already set tongues wagging. There is even talk that Elisha Scott is anxious to find fresh quarters! The international custodian has not been feeling himself of late, and in consequence the directors have given him a rest. The merits of Scott and Riley have always been a debatable subject on Merseyside, but the bulk of the feeling is with Scott, whom Steve Bloomer [the former Derby County and England forward] describes as the best goalkeeper he has ever seen ... but who can forget Scott's wonderful displays? .... It should not be long before Scott is again keeping the fort for his side.

Scott did regain his place, and in 1931-32 he missed only 5 games as Liverpool finished mid-table in the First Division. He finally called it a day in 1934 and there were plenty of tears when he made his farewell speech after Liverpool's final home game of the season. He became player-manager of Belfast Celtic, helping them to Irish League and Cup honours. After the club left the Irish League in 1948, following sectarian violence at a match against Linfield, he was offered the managership of Glenavon but Celtic, now a sort of 'ghost' club, still in existence but not competing, refused to release him. He was 65 when he died in a Belfast hospital in May 1959.

Harry Chambers

Few players have made such an immediate impact as Harry Chambers. In each of the first 5 seasons following the end of the First World War, he was Liverpool's leading scorer. When the Reds won the Football League championship in 1921-22 and then retained the title, Chambers was on target 41 times in 71 games. All told, in 228 League and FA Cup matches for Liverpool he scored 151 goals, an average of almost a goal every 2 games. When he played for England he was just as prolific – 5 goals in 8 internationals.

Born at Willington Quay in Northumberland, Chambers played for England Schoolboys against Scotland and Wales in 1911, when he was 14. He signed for Liverpool from North Shields Athletic, which also produced Arthur Metcalf, who scored 28 goals in 63 games for Liverpool between 1912 and 1915.

On 14 April 1915, the *Liverpool Echo* reported, 'Mr Tom Watson may secure the signature of a smart young inside-left name Henry Chambers. He is only 18 years old and has earned a reputation in North-Eastern League circles … . Chambers weighs 12st 6lbs and stands 5ft 10ins.' The following day, Chambers made his Liverpool debut for the reserve team against Huddersfield Town in the Central League. A week later, reporting on a match between Liverpool reserves and Preston North End reserves, the newspaper's sports columnist Bee said:

> Yesterday I had the delight of seeing some of the young bloods of the Anfield club. Chambers, the Shields man, is built on sturdy lines and is especially smart with his head. He scored a capital goal with a first-time shot, and was quite the soundest footballer of his line. He was in the big naphtha [a flammable liquid hydrocarbon mixture] explosion up

North some time ago, and the wonder is that he is alive to tell the tale. For many months he had to wear a hand-bandage.

Despite his impressive displays for the second team, Chambers had to wait 4 years for his first-team debut. During the First World War, he served in the Connaught Rangers regiment before being invalided home from Salonika in 1917. He then guested for Belfast Distillery and Glentoran. In October 1918, *The Northern Whig* reported that 'Glentoran supporters will be pleased to learn that Chambers, the speedy Liverpool forward, who led the England attack at Windsor Park last Saturday, has arrived and is a certain starter ... he should materially strengthen the Glentoran forward line.'

When his time at Anfield finally came, Chambers scored on his senior debut, in a 3-1 win at Bradford City on 30 August 1919. His goal came just before the interval and the *Liverpool Echo* reporter thought that the 'capital goal ... showed that the inside-right knows how to seize an opportunity'. By the end of that season, Chambers had seized 15 such opportunities in 34 games as Liverpool finished in fourth place in the First Division.

Then came all those remarkable scoring feats until, in 1927-28, he was transferred to West Bromwich Albion where he turned out at centre-half. He was later player-manager of Oakengates Town and Hereford United. In January 1933, Oakengates told Hereford that, unless Chambers moved on (they could no longer afford his wages), they would be unable to fulfil a fixture at Hereford that Saturday. Chambers also ran a pub, worked as a labourer, and played for his local amateur club right up his death in June 1949. He was 52. 'Stork' of the *Liverpool Echo* recalled how:

'Smiler', as he was known to the crowds because there was always a grin on his face, was not only a scorer of goals, but made others play through his astute generalship and amazing football sense ... those who saw him play never forget him, and goalkeepers who had to face up to his shots did so with fear in their hearts, for Chambers, thanks to his 'pigeon toes', could apply swerve to his shots which was most disconcerting ... . He was one of that wonderful trinity of Chambers, Hopkin and Bromilow.

Dick Forshaw

On 19 September 1925, Liverpool beat Manchester United 5-0 at Anfield, where Dick Forshaw scored a hat-trick that afternoon. *Athletic News* described his goals:

> Forshaw, outmanoeuvring Barson and Silcock, found the corner of the net with a strong left-foot drive … . Forshaw deceived both Barson and Moore and put in a right-foot shot at great pace that completely beat Steward, and following a period in which Scott was kept busy, Forshaw obtained his third goal … . Forshaw was the man who caught the eye; his speed, trickiness, uncanny anticipation, and shooting being features that characterised his play throughout.

That season, Forshaw scored 29 goals in 35 League and FA Cup matches. It was his best season for Liverpool, but others were even more valuable to the club. When the Reds won the First Division title in consecutive seasons, 1921-22 and 1922-23, Forshaw never missed a game in either campaign and in 84 League appearances scored a total of 36 goals. The first of his Liverpool career had come on 20 September 1919, at Villa Park. It gave Liverpool a 1-0 win and was 1 of 90 goals in the First and Second Divisions that afternoon. Only 14 were shared between the 17 clubs that failed to gain a point, so Liverpool's win bucked the trend of big victories.

Forshaw, who was born in Lancashire in 1895, served with the Royal Garrison Artillery in Ceylon during the First World War and played wartime football with Nottingham Forest and Middlesbrough before the Reds signed him. The (*Sheffield*) *Star Green 'Un*, reported, 'R. Forshaw, the Liverpool forward whose "loss" Middlesbrough have been deploring, never was registered for the latter, although he signed a form for them last April. Fortunately for club and player it was discovered in time that he was on Liverpool's list, and the second form cancelled.'

In March 1927, Liverpool sold Forshaw to Everton for £3,750. The *Liverpool Echo* said, 'The secret nature will be one of the greatest debated transfers the game has ever known.' Forshaw had scored 124 goals in 287 senior appearances for Liverpool. With Everton, he won another League championship medal before moving to Wolves in 1929. Despite his goal-scoring, he was never selected to play for England. He ended his career with Hednesford Town, Rhyl Athletic and Waterford in the League of Ireland.

In May 1932, Forshaw appeared before Liverpool Quarter Sessions, accused of fraud. One Richard Green had given him £100 to place as much money as he could on Grand Salute to win the Royal Hunt Cup at Ascot. Forshaw placed 3 bets at £2 each way, each time adding a '0' to make it look as though the bets were £20, and keeping the rest of the stake for himself. Had Grand Salute lost, then that would have been the end of the matter. Unfortunately for Forshaw, it won. He fled to France where he worked as coach to a football club. On his return, he was arrested in London. He was defended by no less a barrister than Hartley Shawcross – later the lead British prosecutor at the Nuremberg War Crimes tribunal – who told the court that, during his playing days, Forshaw had accumulated a small sum 'by way of transfer fees and the like' but after a knee injury ended his career, he set up with others as commission agents in Liverpool. The business failed and moneylenders pressed him. His capital exhausted, he took to defrauding Mr Green. He was found guilty and sentenced to 12 months' hard labour.

His troubles did not end there. In November 1933, he pleaded guilty to 4 counts of theft and was sentenced to a further 17 months' hard labour. It became a recurring pattern – released from prison and then reoffending. Hours after leaving prison in 1937, he took silverware from a London hotel before drunkenly stealing 2 suitcases from Euston Railway Station. The magistrate asked him, 'Can't you pull yourself up before it is too late?' Forshaw replied, 'That's what I want to do.'

Dick Forshaw died in 1963.

Tom Bromilow

Writing in the *Liverpool Echo* on Saturday, 7 March 1959, Leslie Edwards said, 'Anfield fans whose memory takes them back to the club's 2 consecutive League championship triumphs of the 1920s will be as sorry as me about the death of the best half-back the club ever had – Tom Bromilow. He died suddenly when travelling back to Leicester from Wrexham on Wednesday.' The former Liverpool favourite was returning from a scouting trip. He was taken from a train at Nuneaton Railway Station and certified dead at the nearby Manor Hospital. He was 64.

A few weeks later, an *Echo* reader, Mr P. A. Tunstall, recalled a game between Liverpool and Arsenal at Anfield on 23 January 1926. Liverpool were winning 3-0 when, in the dying seconds, the referee was hit in the face by the ball. The official managed to hand his whistle to the nearest player, who blew to end the match. 'Carrying the fantasy even further,' commented the *Echo,* 'the referee, T. G. Bryan and the player, Thomas George Bromilow, had the same initials.' In fact, Tommy Bromilow's birth was registered as George Thomas but why let that spoil the story?

There was no fantasy concerning the career of Tommy Bromilow. He made his debut for mid-table Liverpool in October 1919, against third-placed Burnley at Turf Moor, where the Reds won 2-1. He made his final appearance on 3 May 1930, in a 1-0 defeat at Ewood Park where Liverpool went down to what *Athletic News* described as 'a lucky goal scored 2 minutes before the interval' to finish 12th in the First Division. It was Bromilow's 374th appearance for Liverpool. He had scored 11 goals for the Reds.

Tommy Bromilow was a Scouser, the seventh of 8 children and the son of a blacksmith, born in West Derby on 7 October 1894. He played for United West Dingle Presbyterian Club before joining the Army in the First World War. There is a report that, towards the end of the war, he was invalided out because of a septic toe. He turned up at Anfield asking for a trial. That went well and in the first post-war Football League season of 1919-20, he was signed on as a professional. Only 17 months after his first-team debut, he was playing for England. Standing only 5ft 9ins and weighing less than 11st, he was not built for the hard, physical contact normally associated with those who operate in midfield, but he was still a ball-winner, and that, coupled with the ability of find his forwards with defence-splitting passes, made him a vital cog in the title-winning seasons of 1921-22 and 1922-23, when altogether he missed only 3 matches in the First Division.

Before a match against Derby County at the Baseball Ground in February 1928, the *Derby Daily Telegraph* described Bromilow as thus: 'though on the small side so far as weight and muscular strength are concerned, he is wonderfully effective and artistic in all he does ... . No half could play the ball with greater effect.'

Bromilow's England debut came against Wales at Ninian Park in March 1921, and, all told, he won 7 caps, the last at Windsor Park, Belfast, when he was just past his 31st birthday.

After retiring as a player, Bromilow took a coaching job in Amsterdam before becoming Burnley's manager in October 1932. One of his last acts as the Clarets' manager was to sign a teenager called Tommy Lawton. For 1 season, 1935-36, Bromilow was secretary-manager of Crystal Palace. In 1936, he applied for the vacant Liverpool job but the Reds' board favoured George Kay. So, Bromilow went off to Wales to manage Newport County, returning to Palace from 1937 until 1939. Just before the outbreak of the Second World War, he was appointed manager of Leicester City, taking them to several honours during the ersatz years of wartime football. He began a second spell at Newport in 1946, and then in 1950 returned to Leicester City as chief scout. Everton manager Theo Kelly was his brother-in-law.

Tommy Lucas

In October 1916, *Liverpool Echo's* Bee summed up the Reds' defence so far that season:

> Lucas, the junior member, is one of the best 'finds' the war session has brought us. He is awfully like Herbert Burgess, who has always been held up as a model of a full-back. What a rush there has been for his signature. Everton believed they had booked him, but 'scraps of paper' in that day were torn up as ruthlessly as by Wilhelm [the German Kaiser] in recent years. However, that's beside the point … . A rare judge of length, clean in kick, yet daring and dashing, Lucas promises to become an All-England player in the days of peace.

Tommy Lucas was born in St Helens on 22 September 1895, the eighth of 14 children of a coal hewer. He worked as a haulage hand and played for a variety of non-League clubs before making 3 appearances for Manchester United in March 1916, 1 of them a goalless draw against Liverpool at Old Trafford in the wartime Lancashire Section Subsidiary (Southern) tournament. He was on trial but it seems that, although United might have kept him, Lucas saw his future elsewhere.

He made his First Division debut for Liverpool against Aston Villa at Anfield on 13 September 1919. The Reds won 2-1 and the (*Sheffield*) *Star Green 'Un* said, 'Lucas of Liverpool was in grand form, and the home team were the better side.' He made 16 appearances that season, and 29 the next, and when Liverpool won the League championship in 1921-22, he played 27 times. However, when the Reds retained the title in 1922-23, he found himself out of favour as Eph Longworth and Donald McKinlay made the full-back positions their own. McKinlay was ever-present and Longworth missed only 1 game, when he played for England against Scotland at Hampden Park in April. That gave Lucas his only senior appearance of the season, in a 1-1 draw at Huddersfield Town. He was busy that afternoon, the *Liverpool Echo* reporting that 'Huddersfield promptly renewed their aggressive operations until Lucas punted clear ... . Another effort by the home side looked ominous, but Lucas showed his sterling qualities as a defender ... . Another strong attack on the visitors' goal was splendidly saved by Lucas.'

The following season, Lucas and Longworth shared the right-back position, and in 1924-25 he partnered McKinlay for most of the season. In 1925-26, Lucas was absent only 3 times and it was the turn of Longworth, now 38, to stand aside. In 1928-29, it was Lucas who had to make way for a younger player as Jimmy 'The Parson' Jackson – at 27 some 6 years Lucas's junior – never missed a match at right-back while Lucas managed only 5 games, 2 as Jackson's partner on the left, and 3 at centre-half in the final matches of the season after Dave Davidson injured an ankle in a 5-2 win at Derby on 13 April.

Lucas kept bouncing back, however. In 1929-30, he made 31 appearances at left-back, and in 1930-31 was ever-present in that position. But new challengers, such as Bob Done from Runcorn, and Willie Steel from St Johnstone, were making their presence felt. In July 1933, Tommy Lucas moved to Third Division South club Clapton Orient. He had made 366 League and FA Cup appearances for Liverpool, and scored 3 goals. At Orient he joined his former Liverpool teammate David Pratt, the manager at Lea Bridge Road. Pratt moved to manage Notts County in December 1934, by which time Lucas was looking after Orient's nursery club, Ashford Town, in the Kent League. He later managed Aylesbury United. Bee's prediction that he would play for England had borne fruit in October 1921 when he played against Ireland at Windsor Park, Belfast, the first of 3 caps. He captained England in his last international, in Antwerp in 1926. Tommy Lucas died on 11 December 1953. For the past 18 years he had run the Woolsack pub in Stoke Mandeville. He was 58.

Fred Hopkin

The pitch was a sea of mud and at half-time on 3 March 1923, Liverpool led Bolton Wanderers 2-0 at Anfield, through Dick Forshaw and Dick Johnson. The *Liverpool Echo* reported that, 'The ball skidded considerably and outpaced the players, and once, when the ball was out into the spectators, it plumped on to a man's trilby hat and forced the water that had gathered in the ridge up into the air.'

Four minutes after half-time, Liverpool's outside-left, Fred Hopkin, cut in from the left and let fly with a left-foot shot that flew into the right-hand side of Dick Pym's goal. It was Hopkin's first-ever goal for Liverpool, in his 70th League appearance for the Reds. The *Liverpool Echo* said, 'The crowd to a man raised a joyful noise, and for 5 minutes kept up a roar of applause to celebrate this maiden goal.'

Moments later, smoke began to rise from the Anfield Road grandstand. At first it appeared to be nothing serious, but soon the pitch was enveloped. Police cleared spectators from the stand, Hopkin nearly scored a second goal, referee Bearley spoke to Bolton's Ted Vizard, and men from Westminster Road Fire Station tackled the fire. Three-nil down, Bolton looked to having the game abandoned but the fire was doused, the smoke cleared, and Liverpool marched on towards retaining the First Division title. Happily, no one was injured by the fire that *The Sunday Post* said had been caused by either a lit cigarette or match dropped in the stand of which 25 yards of damage was caused. Thus, outside-left Fred Hopkin entered Liverpool football folklore as the player whose goal came as such a surprise that the ground caught fire.

Born in Dewsbury in September 1895, Hopkin played for Darlington in the Northern League and guested for Manchester United during the First World War before signing for United for the first post-war season. He scored 8 goals in 74 League and FA Cup games before Liverpool signed him in late May 1921, the player receiving a share of the

£2,500 transfer fee. In November 1921, United were fined £350 by the Football League for paying Hopkin wages in excess of the maximum allowed and promising him a sum out of the transfer fee also in excess of the sum allowed.

Hopkin was ever-present when Liverpool won the First Division in 1921-22, and he missed only 2 games when they retained the title the following season. There was just the 1 goal, the shot that apparently set Anfield ablaze.

Thereafter he remained a regular in Liverpool's left wing, and altogether made 359 senior appearances – managing 11 goals in total – before being transferred to his first club, Darlington, who were now members of the Third Division North, in August 1931. He had missed only 6 League games for Liverpool in 1930-31, and, even though he was now almost 36 years old, many Reds supporters felt that the club should have kept him for another season at least. Gordon Gunson had been signed from Wrexham to replace Hopkin but was selected only 18 times in the 2 seasons before Hopkin left Anfield. Liverpool had initially put Hopkin on the transfer list at £1,000 but this had gradually been reduced until Darlington paid £100 for him. He had a shop in the Durham town and that almost certainly clinched his decision to move back to Feethams. The *Sunderland Daily Echo and Shipping Gazette* felt that Darlington had secured a bargain for a player who was 'extremely fit owing to being a teetotaller and non-smoker all his life'. *The Lancashire Evening Post* agreed: 'Hopkin is fit enough to go on for 2 or 3 years … loss of hair has not, as with Samson, meant a loss of strength.' The paper felt that although he was famous for scoring very few goals 'he was content to go on putting the ball in middle with the old campaigner's expert touch.'

Hopkin made 26 Football League appearances, scoring 2 goals, for Darlington. He died in Darlington in March 1970, aged 74.

George Patterson

When George Patterson died on 8 May 1955, at the age of 68 after many years of ill-health, it was a sad time for Liverpool. Twenty-four hours earlier, John W. Morris, who had been a director of the club for less than 12 months, had also passed away. Liverpool had been badly hit by the deaths of officials in recent times. Secretary Jack Rouse had died only a few months earlier, and in the past 2 seasons, former manager George Kay and directors Jimmy Troop, Harvey Webb and Ralph K. Milne had also gone.

George Patterson had joined Liverpool as assistant secretary 47 years earlier. When Tom Watson died in 1915, he was appointed secretary, and in 1928, when Matt McQueen resigned as manager, Patterson had taken on the dual role of secretary-manager, holding the joint post until George Kay was appointed in 1936, whereupon Patterson remained as secretary until the Football League was suspended on the outbreak of the Second World War in 1939. He retained his interest in Liverpool, however, and attended games at Anfield regularly until his deteriorating health made that impossible.

Patterson, who was born in Liverpool in 1887, had played non-League football with Marine. After Tom Watson's sudden death, he took over responsibility for team affairs for regional football that was the staple fare for the remainder of the First World War. When the Football League resumed in August 1919, Liverpool appointed David Ashworth, a former referee who had managed Oldham Athletic and Stockport County. Ashworth's 3-year spell at Anfield saw the Reds win the First Division in consecutive seasons, although surprisingly he returned to Oldham Athletic, who were now bottom of the First Division, before the second title was confirmed.

After Ashworth's appointment, Patterson had returned to being Liverpool's secretary only and it was a role in which he continued until

Matt McQueen decided to retire. At that point Patterson took on the manager's job again, although the directors chose the team, leaving Patterson responsible for player recruitment and getting the right results on match days. His record of signing players is impressive. Youngsters such as Jack Balmer and Phil Taylor, who would go on to become great Liverpool names, began their Anfield careers when Patterson was manager, while established stars such as Matt Busby, Tom Cooper and Tom Bradshaw also joined the club while he was in charge.

Unfortunately, after the title triumphs of the early 1920s, Patterson's tenure as Liverpool's manager was far less successful. In his first full season, of 1928-29, the Reds finished fifth, which was a great improvement on the previous season's 16th final place, but after that they were mostly in mid-table, flirting with relegation in 1933-34, when they finished 18th, and coming even closer in 1935-36, when they ended up in 19th place, only 3 points ahead of relegated Aston Villa and 5 ahead of bottom club Blackburn Rovers. Only a slightly better goal average kept them ahead of the 20th club in the table, Sheffield Wednesday. Liverpool won only 3 of their last 20 games of that season.

On 18 July 1936, the *Liverpool Echo* reported that Liverpool intended to advertise for a new manager the following week: 'It is now plain that Mr George Patterson will concentrate upon the task of secretarial work and a new manager will come to Anfield which had had few such men since its inception … . Anfield has never been over-staffed in the office and the decision to split Mr Patterson's duties and bring in a manager has been decided upon.'

In 1946-47, when Liverpool won the League championship again, Jack Balmer and Phil Taylor, those 2 young players whose Anfield careers had begun when Patterson was manager, each made a huge contribution to the success.

George Patterson died at his home in Skerries Road, just a short distance from the Anfield ground, and he was buried in Anfield Cemetery. For decades his grave was unmarked, until a subscription was raised to mark his final resting place with a headstone.

Jimmy McDougall

When George Patterson signed 24-year-old inside-left Jimmy McDougall from Partick Thistle in April 1928, he knew that his new player would not be available until the following season, which was frustrating for the Liverpool manager because the Reds desperately needed points to help in their relegation battle. McDougall had played in every match for Partick Thistle so far that season and scored 26 goals. With 3 games remaining, his power up front would have been more than just useful. But he had been signed too late in the season. In the end, Liverpool drew a Wednesday early evening game at home to Leicester City, beat Tottenham Hotspur 2-0 at Anfield, and, despite losing 6-1 at Old Trafford on the last day of the season, managed to avoid the drop, finishing 16th in a table where only 2 points separated bottom-of-the-table Middlesbrough from 14th-placed Sheffield Wednesday.

McDougall's first game in a Liverpool shirt came in a Central League match at Ewood Park, and he had to wait until 25 August 1928, and a home game against Bury, to make his first-team debut in a 2-0 win. His first goal came in the sixth minute of his second game, at Villa Park where, despite McDougall giving Liverpool an early lead, they went down 3-1. By the end of that season, though, the Reds had climbed to fifth place, and McDougall had missed only 6 games. His goal tally was 8, however, because midway through the season he was switched to left-half – and it was in that position that he was to serve Liverpool with distinction for the next 9 years, during which time he hardly missed a game as the Reds bumped around in the middle of the First Division, now and again flirting with relegation but never challenging for honours. Indeed, their best finishing position when he was at Anfield came in his debut season.

Jimmy McDougall, who was born in Port Glasgow on 23 January 1904, joined Partick Thistle from Port Glasgow Athletic Juniors in 1925, although he did not immediately establish himself in Thistle's senior team. It was that fine run of form in 1927-28 that finally brought him to the attention of the leading English clubs, and which led him to Liverpool, where, with Matt Busby on the right and Tom 'Tiny' Bradshaw at centre-half, he would form one of the best half-back lines the club has ever had.

In May 1931, McDougall was called up for Scotland's matches, in Vienna and Rome. Without any players from Celtic, Rangers and Motherwell, and with an injury to East Fife's Danny Liddle leaving the Scots with only 10 men, they lost 5-0 to Austria in the Hohe Warte Stadium. McDougall must have done reasonably well because he was made captain for the next match, against Italy in the Stadio Nazionale, watched by Benito Mussolini. Writing in *The Scotsman*, the Rev Albert G. Mackinnon said, 'I had a front view of Italy's greatest statesman during the whole game and divided my attention between him and it.' Scotland lost again, this time 3-0, and although there was some damage repair with a 3-2 against Switzerland in Geneva, McDougall had already played in his last international.

He made his final appearances for Liverpool on 15 January 1938, at The Valley where Charlton Athletic won 3-0. At the end of Liverpool's match against Aston Villa at Anfield on 15 October 1938, he was presented with a benefit cheque from the club for £650. After 357 senior appearances for the Reds, and 12 goals, two-thirds of them coming in his first season, he became player-coach of South Liverpool FC, from where he retired on the eve of the Second World War, when he was 35. He then ran a successful chandlery business and died in the city in July 1984. He left a widow, a daughter and 2 grandchildren.

In March 1940, he had told *The Liverpool Evening Express*, 'Coming to Anfield was the best move I ever made. I thoroughly enjoyed all the years I had with the club.'

Gordon Hodgson

On 1 October 1924, the South African touring team arrived at Anfield to play a Liverpool 11. They surprised the locals by winning 5-2 and the *Daily Herald* reported that 'although Liverpool made some bright attacks just before half-time, they were completely outplayed subsequently.' Star of the afternoon was inside-forward Gordon Hodgson, a 20 year old from Johannesburg, who scored a hat-trick. Two weeks later, *Athletic News* was still raving about him: 'A forward who is much talked about is Gordon Hodgson, who had been playing at inside-right ... . Fast and clever, he is a fine shot ... he is regarded as a footballer of great possibilities.'

Inevitably, Hodgson caught the eye of several clubs – Chelsea's long-serving manager, David Calderhead, felt that the 2 goals the South African had scored at Stamford Bridge were just about the best he had ever seen – but it was Liverpool who signed him in November 1925, when *Athletic News* said that it was 'believed that if properly "nursed" he might make a big name in English football. He is expected to leave Cape Town this month.' Four months earlier, Arthur Riley, Hodgson's goalkeeping colleague on the tour had also signed for Liverpool, to cover for Elisha Scott.

Hodgson, a boilermaker by trade, was born to English parents. He made his senior debut for Liverpool against Manchester City at Maine Road on 27 February 1926. The *Liverpool Echo* was impressed: 'Goodchild had to spring quickly across the goal to capture a header from Hodgson ... McNab, Hodgson and Oxley joined hands in a beautiful bit of combination.' The game ended 1-1, and Hodgson retained his place for the next 11 games until he missed the last 2 matches of the season, through injury after colliding with Blackburn Rovers' Aussie Campbell at Anfield.

Hodgson was in the team from the start of the following season, and there he remained for the next 10 years, not only establishing himself as one of the First Division's best players, but winning England caps as well. In 1928-29, as Liverpool finished fifth, he scored 30 goals which included 2 hat-tricks – 1 in the first half of a 4-4 draw against Arsenal at Highbury, and 1 in an 8-0 thrashing of Burnley at Anfield on Boxing Day. The 1930-31 season was his best, though: a club record 36 goals with hat-tricks against Chelsea, Sheffield United and Blackpool, all at home, and 4 goals in a 5-3 win at Hillsborough where Sheffield Wednesday were chasing a hat-trick of League championship titles.

Hodgson's England debut came in October 1930, against Ireland at Bramall Lane, and he won 2 more caps, against Wales at Wrexham the following month, and at Hampden Park in March 1931. He scored 1 goal for England.

Hodgson scored 240 goals in 378 senior games for Liverpool. His 232 League goals were a club record until Roger Hunt surpassed it some 30 years later, although, unlike Hunt's goals, all of Hodgson's were scored in the First Division.

In January 1936, Liverpool transferred him to Aston Villa for £3,000, and he moved on to Leeds United in March 1937. He ended his playing career during the Second World War, in which he coached the young players at Elland Road, briefly guested for York City and worked in a munitions factory in Leeds. In October 1946, Hodgson, who also played 56 times for Lancashire, helping them to win the County Cricket Championship in 1928 and 1930, was appointed manager of Port Vale, a post he held until his death, from inoperable throat cancer, at his home in Burslem on 14 June 1951. He was 47.

When George Kay retired as Liverpool manager in 1951, Hodgson had applied for the job and was 1 of a shortlist of 6 that the club interviewed before deciding on Don Welsh. On his death, Liverpool's chairman, George Richards, said, 'We remember with pride the great service that Gordon Hodgson gave Liverpool. He was a grand sportsman, always a genuine trier, and never gave us a moment's anxiety.'

Arthur Riley

Like his Springbok teammate Gordon Hodgson, goalkeeper Arthur Riley caught Liverpool's eye when he played for the South African touring team at Anfield in February 1924. The Reds just had to sign them both. It was Riley who arrived back at Anfield first, sailing from Cape Town in July 1925, along with the tourists' centre-forward, David Murray, who was bound for Goodison Park. Liverpool saw the 21-year-old Riley as cover for the great Elisha Scott and initially that proved to be the case as the South African was restricted to 3 appearances in his first season, coming in only when Scott was injured.

In the *Daily Herald*, columnist 'Syrian' mischievously asked what would happen if the Football League decreed that no club should play a man born outside a 10-mile radius of the club's headquarters: 'Liverpool would be deprived of their 2 goalkeepers, Scott (Belfast) and Riley (South Africa) but could call on Taylor (Huddersfield) and Howard Baker (Chelsea). Chambers would have to go to South Shields or Newcastle.' It was an interesting point as Syrian redistributed footballers according to where they were born. Fortunately, the League had no such plans and Scott and Riley remained at Anfield.

It would be 2 seasons before Riley established himself in the Liverpool first team, and 1929-30 before he was the first-choice goalkeeper. Then, for some reason, he lost form and it was 1933-34 before he was again first pick. In 1934-35 and 1935-36 he missed only 2 games each season. But he was dropped in favour of Alf Hobson, who had been signed from Shildon Colliery, and then his fellow South African, Dirk Kemp, took over. It seemed that George Kay and the Liverpool board could never quite make up their minds about Arthur Riley, but he still made 338 appearances for the Reds.

On 23 September 1939, Riley made his first appearance of the season, against Bolton Wanderers in a wartime friendly match at Anfield.

Riley was coming back after dislocating a finger in the Reds' second practice match of the season and he replaced Kemp who had himself just undergone a minor operation on his left hand. On 2 October, Liverpool beat Blackburn Rovers 5-0 in another friendly, this time at Ewood Park. The *Liverpool Daily Post* commented, 'Riley and his full-backs were so obviously on top form that Blackburn's efforts looked puny.'

Fit again, Sergeant Dirk Kemp returned for a few games but was then sent on an Army course in the south of England and declared unavailable for the remainder of the season. On 11 February 1940, Riley, now also serving as a sergeant in an infantry regiment, kept goal for the British Army against the French Army in Paris. In the *Liverpool Echo*, columnist 'Ranger' wrote, 'I am particularly pleased to see Arthur Riley honoured again. The Liverpool man has had to wait a long time for his merits to be recognised, but in the 2 representative games he has played this season he has shown the powers-that-be what a brilliant custodian he is.' Other representative honours followed, including an appearance, along with Liverpool's Matt Busby, for an All British XI against the Football League at Bradford, in aid of the Red Cross in February 1940. In April 1942, *The Liverpool Evening Express* reported that Riley, 'one of 27 Liverpool players who joined up before the war', had risen to the rank of company sergeant major but was now discharged from further service and 'back in Civvy Street and anxious to do all he can to further the war effort.'

On 5 June 1944, the eve of D-Day, *Good Morning*, the daily newspaper produced for the Royal Navy's submarine branch, remembered Riley as being 'lithe as a panther' in Liverpool's goal before the war. In January 1950, Riley was running a sports outfitter in the small town of Boksburg, about 16 miles from Johannesburg. In March 1988, the *Liverpool Echo* reported that Riley, then 84, had recently been unwell but was recovering from a stomach operation in Boksburg-Benoni Hospital in Johannesburg.

Jimmy Jackson

It was inevitable that Jimmy Jackson should be known as 'The Parson'. Besides being an excellent footballer, he was also an erudite man who studied divinity in order to become a minister. When Jackson died in January 1977, Leslie Edwards, former sports editor of the *Liverpool Echo*, recalled that Jackson's real ambition was not to play for England but to become a clergyman, and so, when he joined Liverpool in May 1925, he made it clear that while he intended to remain at Anfield for some seasons, he would concurrently be studying for the ministry. Edwards wrote, 'The arrangement worked well. He soon found a place in the first team and there he stayed until his playing days ended. When denizens of Spion Kop learned of his remarkable extra-curricular activities, they named him "Parson" Jackson.'

When he signed for Liverpool from Aberdeen, Dundee's *Evening Telegraph* reported that 'the news will cause a sensation as Jackson has been one of the most consistently successful players on the club's books, and following the departure of Alex Jackson [who had moved to Huddersfield Town for a club record £5,000 fee] and the absence of any notable signings, his transfer will not be welcomed locally'. The paper explained:

> Jackson was officially announced as having signed for Aberdeen for next season, and on the strength of his displays for the team at either half-back or back, the news gave general satisfaction and the announcement that he has now been signed for Liverpool will not please supporters of the Pittodrie club. Jackson, who is the son of an old Scottish internationalist, joined Aberdeen from Motherwell 2 seasons ago. Previously, he was associated with Queen's Park. He is one of the few English-born players who have been capped for Scotland.

In fact Jackson, who was born in Newcastle upon Tyne in December 1900, never played for Scotland, although he had represented the Scottish League. His father was a former Woolwich Arsenal captain, and a cousin, Archie, played Test cricket for Australia.

Jackson cost Aberdeen £2,000 when he signed from Motherwell in June 1923, and they initially wanted £4,500 from Liverpool but settled on £1,750 for the centre-half who wanted away. He had worked in a shipyard and in an office before becoming a full-time footballer, 'all grit and determination' according to a contemporary account, and began his university studies while with Aberdeen, continuing them while with Liverpool – at St Aidan's College in Birkenhead, and, from 1931, at Cambridge University – which meant that he occasionally missed chunks of the season. In 1928, he was invited to become the assistant minister at Liverpool's Shaw Street Presbyterian Church. He later worked on the Isle of Man and was president of the Liverpool Free Church Council. For 8 years until he retired in 1963, Jackson was minister of Bournemouth Presbyterian Church.

For Liverpool, he proved to be a versatile player, mostly in defence but also in midfield, and he captained the Reds, making 224 appearances – and scoring 2 goals – before leaving the game following his ordination in 1933. Jackson's final game was at Huddersfield on 18 April of that year. During an injury crisis, he stepped up for the first time since mid-February. Liverpool lost 3-1 but not before Jackson had equalised with a 'brilliant goal' according to the *Yorkshire Post and Leeds Intelligencier*. He had to look back to December 1928, and a 3-1 defeat at White Hart Lane, for his only other Liverpool goal, 'a smart shot at short range after a corner-kick', according to *The Scotsman*.

The FA Cup provided 1 of his greatest moments with Liverpool. On 9 January 1932, the Reds fell a goal behind after only 45 seconds' play in a third-round tie at Goodison Park when Dixie Dean took advantage of a slip-up between Tom Bradshaw and Tom Morrison. Then, before half-time, Gordon Gunson levelled the scores, Gordon Hodgson scored the winner, and it was Jimmy Jackson who made the difference, shackling Dean and, according to *The* (Dundee) *Courier*, 'forced a sorry team into a successful team by his pulpit power'.

Tom Bradshaw

When Manchester United arrived at Anfield on 25 January 1930, they were still talking about the surprise signing that Liverpool had pulled off the previous day. Tom Bradshaw, a Scottish international centre-half, had joined the Reds from Bury for a fee reported to be £7,600 or possibly even more; the British record of £10,890 had been set 2 years earlier when Arsenal signed David Jack from Bolton, so the money for Bradshaw was up there with some of the highest ever paid at the time and certainly a Liverpool club record. Two Liverpool officials had worked nearly all night to complete his signing.

For a big man – he stood 6ft 1¾ins and was known as 'Tiny' – Bradshaw was a skilful player. Reporting on his debut, against relegation-threatened United, the *Liverpool Echo* said:

> Naturally, Bradshaw was closely watched, but the first thing he did was done in the manner of an artist … Bradshaw was tackled by a rival, but by putting his boot on top of the ball he made that rival look silly and then went on to offer Hopkin the choicest of choice passes … some of Bradshaw's work was delightful. He was cool in all circumstances.

Liverpool won 1-0 with a 44th-minute goal from Harry Race in a game spoiled by United's offside tactics.

Tom Bradshaw was born in Bishopton, Renfrewshire, on 7 February 1904. He played for Woodside Juniors in the North West Lanarkshire League before joining Bury, then a mid-table Second Division club, in July 1922. He won his only Scotland cap while with the Shakers, and what a game it was for the 'Wembley Wizards' in their 5-1 defeat of England in March 1928. He helped Bury to promotion and left them for Liverpool only after they had dropped back into the second tier.

He missed many games through injury. Three weeks before he signed for the Reds, *The* (Dundee) *Courier* reported:

> Bury find balm in the fact that the luckless Tom Bradshaw has come back, is strong, and shows such that he is qualifying for another Wembley show as he had in that famous victory 2 years ago. Tom was bothered by an injury that no one could solve or dissolve. He finally went to the best footballers' hospital in the world, in Liverpool, and now he owes not any man, nor yet fears any man, which is good news for Scotland and Bury.

Only a few days before his move to Anfield, the same newspaper reported:

> Greater delight comes from the fact that Tom Bradshaw is carrying on. There was serious talk recently about this international player being 'done'. He was injured again. Now we find him in prime order. He played one of those domineering, dominating games at Southampton on a ground that does not exactly suit so big a man ... yet Bradshaw practically took all the honours.

If there was any doubt in Liverpool's mind that Bradshaw's best days were behind him, they were dispelled by reports like this. Five days later, he was a Liverpool player. All those injury worries now behind him, he was ever-present in 1931-32, missed only 6 matches in the following 2 seasons, and altogether ran up 291 League and FA Cup appearances for the Reds. He scored 4 goals, the first coming on 3 September 1932, at St James's Park where Newcastle United were winning 3-0 at half-time. Hodgson scored from the penalty spot for Liverpool after 47 minutes, 8 minutes later, Ted Crawford pulled back another goal, but then Newcastle scored again. There were only seconds remaining when Bradshaw opened his account, too late, alas, to save a point.

In September 1938, Bradshaw signed for South Liverpool. He was now 34 and had made only 2 appearances for Liverpool the previous season. His contract allowed him to move if another League club came for him, and over that same weekend he signed for Third Lanark. He rejoined South Liverpool in July 1939, and later scouted for Norwich City. Tom Bradshaw died in Coatbridge on 22 February 1986. He was 82.

Tom Cooper

It was a fine performance for Port Vale against Derby County in the FA Cup that persuaded Rams manager George Jobey to sign Tom Cooper for £2,500 in March 1926. Jobey was a good judge. Cooper went on to become one of the most polished full-backs in the country. He was capped 15 times for England while he was at the Baseball Ground, and would have won more but for a series of injuries, including ones that resulted in him having cartilages removed from both knees. He captained Derby and he captained England, and he had made 266 League and FA Cup appearances, and scored 1 goal before Liverpool reportedly paid around £7,500 for him in December 1934, when he was 30.

Cooper – known to his teammates as 'Snowy' due to his very fair hair – made his debut for the Reds at Stamford Bridge on 8 December 1934. It was not a happy start. Liverpool lost 4-2. The *Liverpool Echo* said:

> Cooper began his Liverpool service at a moment when the Liverpool Football Club players had a slothful mood and lacked sparkle and punch in front of goal … . Cooper was early in the business of defence, and the strength of his heading out and his pace surprised Gibson [Chelsea inside-forward George Gibson].

His goalkeeper at Derby, Harry Wilkes, said, years later, that if Cooper had a weakness, it was probably when the ball was in the air, but this was apparently not the case when he made his Liverpool bow.

Meanwhile, the *Echo*'s columnist Bee summed it up:

> Cooper – ah – everyone wants to know how he shaped. He had cost £6,800, it is said, and he was on trial far from the Anfield ground. He found working arrangements with his

half-back a trifle difficult to understand. It was natural that he should take time to fit in with a new idea of defence, but his kicking was of grand length and he times his punts to perfection. He was rounded by a swift winger, as many will be, especially if the back is left to take a wing on his own. Two men should always beat one. That was Cooper's fate; his sharp insistent tackling shows he is still the really strong back ... I would say that Cooper made a good debut, but not outstanding.

Cooper missed only 2 of the remaining games of that season, and only injury to an instep kept him out the following season when he played 26 times as Liverpool fought against relegation from the First Division. That was pretty much the pattern of his time at Anfield as Liverpool slowly recovered to finish mid-table in the last 2 seasons before the Second World War. Cooper was also an excellent golfer who regularly won the Merseyside Professional Footballers' Golf Championship.

He had made 160 senior appearances for Liverpool by the time war broke out and the Football League was suspended. He guested for Wrexham in the first wartime season. He was living in Walton, and, like 26 of his colleagues, together with manager George Kay and assistant secretary Jack Rouse, he had enlisted in the Territorial Army the previous May. Liverpool were the first club to join up en bloc.

On 25 June 1940, while serving as a regimental police sergeant-instructor in The King's Regiment (Liverpool), Tommy Cooper was killed near Aldeburgh in Suffolk. The motorcycle that he had been riding was in a head-on-collision with a double-decker bus. He was 35. A verdict of death by misadventure was returned at the inquest, which heard that when it was 40 yards from the bus, the motorcycle seemed to develop a fault. Its front wheel began to wobble and it swerved into the oncoming vehicle. The *Liverpool Daily Post* said, 'A great favourite at Anfield, where he had figured as captain, Cooper's untimely end will be regretted by all followers of the game. Always a dominating figure on the field, his play was entertaining and his kicking and tackling sure. He was one of the most reliable defenders England has produced.'

Alf Hanson

For most of his adult life, Alf Hanson did his best not to use his first given name. It was Adolf. Born in Bootle on 27 February 1912, when the future Führer was allegedly spending a few improbable months in Liverpool as a 23-year-old drop-out art student, Hanson had a trial with Everton before Liverpool signed him in November 1931. A fast outside-left with a reputation for dropping pinpoint crosses on to the heads of Liverpool centre-forwards, or for Berry Nieuwenhuys to meet coming in from the opposite wing, he was a plumber by trade. His brother, Stan, kept goal for Bolton Wanderers from 1935 to 1956.

Alf Hanson made his Liverpool debut on 21 January 1933, coming into the side at Villa Park after a 'flu bug ruled out Gordon Gunson. It was not the happiest of first appearances: Villa won 5-2. In the next League game, at home to Middlesbrough on 1 February, Hanson scored his first goal for Liverpool, but it came in a 3-1 defeat. Ten days later, however, it was a very different story. After being a goal behind – scored by Dixie Dean after Tom Bradshaw lost him – soon after the start of their game against Everton at Anfield, Liverpool were 3-0 ahead, with 1 of the goals coming from Hanson in the 22nd minute, his second for the Reds. Liverpool ran out 7-4 winners.

Injury kept Hanson out of the side for most of 1935-36, but, apart from that, he was a first-choice, and an ever-present in 1936-37. When he signed for Chelsea in the close season of 1938, Liverpool received a club record incoming fee of £7,500. Hanson had scored 52 goals in 177 League and FA Cup games for Liverpool. Chelsea, though, did not get value for money, thanks to the other Adolf. Hanson made only 43 senior appearances, scoring 9 goals, before Hitler invaded Poland, war was declared on Germany, and the Football League closed down for the duration. Hanson continued to play regional football as a guest for various clubs in the north of England, including Liverpool,

New Brighton, Chester, Wrexham, Manchester City, Bolton Wanderers, Crewe Alexandra, Rochdale, Tranmere Rovers and Southport. He also played in a wartime international for England, against Scotland at Newcastle when he partnered West Ham United's Len Goulden on the left wing in a 3-2 defeat by the Scots. In 1945, Hanson became player-manager of South Liverpool, and he also played for and managed Shelbourne United in the League of Ireland, and held a similar post with Ellesmere Port Town. In his younger days, he played cricket and was capped for England at baseball in 1934. Alf Hanson died in October 1993, in hospital in St Helens. He was 81.

In June 1936, the *Liverpool Echo* reported that Liverpool had returned home from their end-of-season trip to the Balkans: 'They won 4 of their 6 matches, and Hanson missed scoring in only one match.' Ernie Blenkinsop told of the final match of the tour, a 2-1 win against Ripensia in Bucharest:

> The players are sort of caged in from the spectators, the reason for which we found out later. It is not unusual for spectators here to take exception to the play and single out an individual in their local derbies for abuse and rough usage ... . The game looked like ending in a draw until 7 minutes from the end when Alf Hanson, from the centre-forward position, lobbed a 'Nivvy' [Nieuwenhuys] centre well wide of the goalie and we ran off worthy winners. After the game, the ground was surrounded by an angry mob waiting for the referee, but, after a while, the official quietened them. This is a feather in Liverpool's cap. Ripensia have only lost one point on this ground, and that to the Austrian international team in a 3-3 draw. So you can imagine all the Liverpool party are very proud. We have a few hours' stay before the Orient Express picks us up, and then, 'Home James, and don't spare the horses'.

Jack Balmer

On 9 November 1946, Jack Balmer scored a hat-trick for Liverpool in their 3-0 win over Portsmouth at Anfield. Seven days later, the Reds beat Derby County 4-1 at the Baseball Ground and Balmer scored all 4 of his side's goals. A week after that, Arsenal lost 4-2 at Anfield – and Balmer scored another 3, making 10 goals in 3 matches. Another week and there was another Balmer goal, this time at Bloomfield Road where Liverpool lost 3-2. Had Albert Stubbins not popped in a 78th-minute effort against Arsenal, that would have been 11 goals for Balmer without another Liverpool player finding the back of the net. As it was, it was still 10 on the trot without anyone else scoring.

There were a few other stumbles for Liverpool in that first post-war season, not least 4 defeats in succession around new year, but they won the League championship for the first time since 1922-23. At the end of the season – which, thanks to an appalling winter, went on into the middle of June before the title was settled – Balmer had scored 24 goals in 39 games to finish as the Reds' joint top scorer alongside Albert Stubbins.

Jack Balmer had joined Liverpool back in May 1935, and so had lost perhaps the best years of his career to the Second World War. He was born in Liverpool on 6 February 1916, and it was no surprise Everton spotted his potential when he was playing for Liverpool's Collegiate Old Boys' team. Two of his uncles, Walter and Robert, had formed a famous full-back pairing at Goodison Park before the First World War. Although he had been scoring freely for his old boys' team, Jack Balmer did not do enough to impress Everton, who let him go after 2 seasons with them on amateur forms. Liverpool had no such reservations and snapped him up. Everton no doubt eventually began to regret their decision. Especially when he scored after only 30 seconds of a Merseyside derby at Goodison Park on 16 February 1938.

Strangely, Liverpool's fans did not entirely warm to him. One theory was that he was too 'middle-class'. Another was that, despite his goals, he lacked the spirit that they liked to see in their forwards, at least the ones who went into the thick of the goalmouth action.

Balmer was ever-present in the last pre-war season of 1938-39, and in the 4 seasons in which he had appeared up to the outbreak of the war, he had scored 34 goals in 122 League games. Overall it was a decent return but it seemed that the prolific centre-forward of his youthful days had given way to a more thoughtful inside-forward.

On 18 November 1939, he played in an unofficial wartime international against Wales at the Recreation Ground, Wrexham, and scored 1 of England's goals in their 3-2 win. Commenting on his selection, the *Liverpool Echo* said that it was deserved: 'His two big assets, in addition to inherent football skill, are quickness off the mark and a willingness to have a bang at goal … if his attempts sometimes … finish up more than a trifle over the bar, I would rather see that than a man who is afraid to shoot at all.'

In January 1940, Balmer was admitted to hospital in Leicester suffering from a stomach illness but recovered to play for Liverpool and to guest for both Brighton and Newcastle United. In March 1944, he was back in hospital, 'indisposed' after receiving a knee in the back playing for the Army at Stoke. In July, it was announced that he could resume playing after a summer's rest.

He captained Liverpool, and when he retired in 1952, had scored 111 goals in 312 senior games. He coached at Anfield until 1955, when he left to concentrate on his business interests.

Jack Balmer died suddenly in Liverpool on Christmas Day 1984, aged 68. His former strike partner, Albert Stubbins, said, 'He was a really good fellow and a fine footballer.'

Berry Nieuwenhuys

On 16 September 1933, Berry Nieuwenhuys made his Central League debut for Liverpool Reserves against Manchester United Reserves at Old Trafford. The *Liverpool Echo* commented:

> Nieuwenhuys is a second edition of Arthur Riley, and is perhaps a stronger sort of player. He is an even-time man, but he had few chances to show his speed on this occasion. There is no mistaking his football skill, however, and everything he did was methodical. He has some tricks, this right-winger, is an ideal centerer of the ball, putting it square and out of the goalkeeper's reach ... . He pulls the ball back well so that there is little chance of the goalkeeper getting an easy catch ... he is sure to make a good partner for Hodgson, should he get the chance.

That chance soon came, just 7 days later in fact, against Tottenham Hotspur. The *Daily Herald* reported:

> Spectators at White Hart Lane on Saturday will see one of South Africa's star footballers in action for Nieuwenhuys (pronounced Nivvenhouse), who only arrived in this country on Monday of last week, has been chosen to play for Liverpool, who will be Hotspur's visitors. Nieuwenhuys, who comes in for Taylor, has not yet appeared at Anfield. He played ... at Old Trafford last Saturday and at Preston on Monday, revealing himself [to be] a fleet-footed, elusive player, and an adept at inter-changing positions. He will have as his partner a fellow South African in Hodgson.

Liverpool won 3-0 that day with goals from Sam English (2) and Alf Hanson. The *Daily Herald* reporter was impressed: 'Liverpool's South Africans are going to help the club to big success. Nieuwenhuys, the outside-right, was splendid, and has already been nicknamed "Nivvy" ... this is a sign of the popularity which he will enjoy when he becomes fully known at Liverpool.'

A week later, Nieuwenhuys scored his first goal for the Reds, in a 3-2 win over Everton. The *Daily Herald* reported that in 'the greatest-ever game combining glorious football, pulsating thrills and brilliant endeavour ... Nieuwenhuys made moves and passes not seen at Anfield for many a long day'.

Alas, Liverpool were to enjoy no success in the years leading up to the Second World War. Eighteenth in Nivvy's first season, then seventh, but then a relegation-haunted 19th, then 18th again, and 2 seasons of finishing 11th before the Football League closed down until 1946. The player prospered, though, with 73 goals – some quite spectacular – in 238 League and FA Cup games up to the war. He worried defenders with his speed, and could play on either wing. In February 1939, after the home match against Everton, Liverpool chairman William Harrop presented him with a benefit cheque for £650.

Berry Nieuwenhuys was born on 5 November 1911 in Kroonstad in the Orange Free State. He worked as an engineer and played for Boksburg and for Germiston Caledonian Society in the Transvaal League before following other South African footballers to Anfield. During the war, Nieuwenhuys served in the RAF and guested for Arsenal and West Ham United.

When the FA Cup resumed in 1945-46, he played in both legs of Liverpool's third-round tie against Chester, and in the fourth round against Bolton Wanderers, scoring in the second leg at Anfield but too late to do anything about turning around a 5-0 first-leg defeat at Burnden Park. When Liverpool won the first post-war League championship, he was 35 and played 15 times and scored 5 goals, but he did not appear in the Reds' run to the 1946-47 FA Cup semi-final. He retired in 1947, having scored 79 goals in 260 senior games for Liverpool.

Two years later, he returned to South Africa where he became assistant golf professional to world-famous Bobby Locke at Transvaal Country Club. In June 1957, he was presented with a memento to mark his work as coach, trainer and masseur to football in Natal. In his day, he had also proved to be a talented baseball and tennis player. Berry Nieuwenhuys died in South Africa in June 1984, after a prolonged illness. He was 72.

George Kay

In early August 1936, George Kay confirmed his appointment as Liverpool's new manager. Still on holiday on the Isle of Wight, in a telephone conversation with Bee, the *Liverpool Echo* columnist, Kay said:

> I am proud to have been offered this post. I don't suggest that I shall win cups and everything else in my path, but I shall do my utmost, and I shall hope to find some more players like Drake of the Arsenal, Light of West Brom, and some others like Holt, who have been found for Southampton. I shall give every encouragement to the boys of the city and its surrounds. It is my first plan to have matches 3 nights a week at Anfield to try to size up any boy who is worth nursing.

Liverpool's chairman, William Harrop, said, 'We have made our decision but Mr Kay just desires time to let his present board consider his position. I expect that Mr Kay will be down at Anfield in 3 weeks' time.'

Bee went on to explain:

> George Kay is a strong fellow, big and powerful, and he has had to work with locals in the Hampshire area, and, moreover, he has had to sell out every year for the purpose of keeping the finance of the [Southampton] club sound. Every year one had to go. It was Drake one year ... . They always had to sell and, having sold, had to proceed to dig out some new talent and frame this for future selling-off periods.'

It was clear why George Kay fancied a move to a club like Liverpool, where good players were bought not sold.

Manchester-born Kay had begun his own playing career with Eccles, then in 1911, when he was 20, moved to Bolton Wanderers. A centre-half, his career at Burnden Park was short and he was soon on his way to the Belfast club, Distillery. During the First World War, he served in the Royal Garrison Artillery before signing for West Ham United in 1919. In 1923, he captained the Hammers against Bolton in the first FA Cup final to be held at Wembley – the famous 'White Horse final' – and made 259 senior appearances for West Ham before ending his playing days with Stockport County. He then managed Luton Town, and kept Southampton in the Second Division for 5 seasons, despite always having to sell the Saints' best players.

At Anfield he took over from George Patterson after the Liverpool board decided to split the posts of manager and secretary, with Patterson concentrating on the latter. In truth, Kay achieved little with the Reds in the years leading up to the Second World War, but during the war he helped keep the club going with the help of some excellent guest players whom he persuaded to turn out, despite long journeys often being involved. In 1946, he suggested that the team visit the United States and Canada, where they would enjoy a better diet than was possible as food rationing became even more severe at home than it had been in wartime.

Thus fortified, Liverpool returned to lift the League championship in 1946-47. The season was disrupted by bad weather but, after the big freeze, Liverpool dropped only 1 point in their last 8 matches to take the title. They also went as far as the FA Cup semi-final where they lost to Burnley at Maine Road. In 1950, despite being ill, Kay led the Liverpool team to Wembley where they lost the Cup final to Arsenal. He had decided to drop Bob Paisley, which arguably cost Liverpool the match, although Paisley praised the way his manager laid the foundations for how Liverpool would play in future.

In February 1951, Kay, who used up a considerable amount of nervous energy every match, 'playing' each ball himself, was advised to retire on medical grounds. Three years later, in April 1954, he died. Billy Liddell said, 'Football will be the poorer for his passing, but the players will be the richer for his teaching.'

Willie Fagan

There was great excitement around Anfield in late October 1937, when it was announced that Liverpool had paid £8,000 to sign 20-year-old inside-forward, Willie Fagan, from Preston North End. It was, said the *Liverpool Echo*, the biggest fee ever paid for a player so young. The signing came at a time when Liverpool supporters needed a fillip after 2 seasons of seeing their favourites flirt with relegation. Liverpool had paid that kind of money before, for Matt Busby, Tom Bradshaw and Sam English. As for Preston, it was the biggest fee they had received since Arsenal bought Alex James.

Fagan had joined Preston from Glasgow Celtic a year earlier, for £3,500, but a run at outside-right did not suit his style, and so he was moved inside, either on the right or the left, and kept his place, right through to North End's appearance in the 1937 FA Cup final, where they lost 3-1 to Sunderland at Wembley. In 36 appearances for Preston, Fagan had scored just 5 goals. He was a better schemer than he was marksman and if he had a fault then, according to the *Liverpool Echo*, it lay in a tendency to be too individualistic, 'but he is unquestionably a ball-player of exceptional gifts. He can dribble a ball around the proverbial sixpence, can beat a man in 2 or 3 ways, and has sufficient resource to develop with experience into an outstanding player.'

After playing 6 times at inside-left at the start of the 1937-38 season, Fagan lost his place to Bobby Beattie, Preston's new signing from Kilmarnock, but the Deepdale club still did not want to sell him, despite having a wealth of talent at inside-forward. Fagan, though, wanted first-team football, and Liverpool could offer him that straight away. He made his debut against Leicester City at Anfield on 23 October. Also making his bow that day was 18-year-old John Shafto, signed from Hexham FC for £10. Their inclusion brought the number of players tried so far by Liverpool that season to 23. According to newspaper reports it was Shafto who made the greater impression in a 1-1 draw.

A week later, in a 3-2 win at Roker Park, Fagan scored his first goal for Liverpool when he took advantage of a slip by Sunderland's Bert Johnston. That season Fagan scored 9 goals in 36 League and FA Cup appearances. In 1938-39, his 14 goals (which included 4 penalties) in 39 League games made him Liverpool's joint top scorer along with Berry Nieuwenhuys and Phil Taylor.

During the Second World War, Fagan, who served in the RAF, was capped by Scotland in 3 unofficial internationals and guested for Aldershot, Leicester City, Northampton Town, Newcastle United, Chelsea, Millwall and Reading. In September 1941, while home on leave, Fagan was down to guest for Celtic but was told at the last minute that, if he did, Liverpool might not be able to call on his services again that season. A few weeks later, however, he was allowed to play for his old club, against Rangers and Clyde.

When the FA Cup resumed in 1945-46, Fagan scored 3 goals in Liverpool's 4 matches, and when the Reds won the League championship in 1946-47, he was on target 7 times in 18 League matches, 2 of them coming in a memorable 7-4 win over Chelsea at Anfield in September. Injuries saw him play less than half the games of the following 2 seasons but in 1949-50, he scored 11 goals in 35 League games, and his 4 FA Cup goals helped Liverpool to the final that season. He played his last game for the Reds in September 1951, at home to Huddersfield, to take his total for to 185 appearances. He scored 57 goals for Liverpool. He played for Belfast Distillery in the Irish League and then became player-manager of Southern League Weymouth Town.

After leaving football, Willie Fagan worked in the prison service. He died at his home in Northampton in February 1992, aged 75, after a long illness.

Cyril Done

On 2 September 1939, 18-year-old Bootle boy Cyril Done marked his debut for Liverpool by scoring a first-half header from a corner against Chelsea at Anfield. It was sufficient to see Liverpool home, despite having right-back Jim Harley sent off in the second half. As Harley trudged towards the dressing room, a spectator ran onto the pitch and made for the referee. A policeman got to the fan first and escorted him from the ground.

Even that incident paled into insignificance against the bigger picture. Almost all the Liverpool team were serving in the Territorial Army and had been on duty as late as 5.00 am on the day of the match before managing to persuade enough colleagues to stand in for them on sentry duty so they got to Anfield in time to play against Chelsea. The *Liverpool Daily Post* reported, 'Liverpool won a gallant victory … but it was an occasion memorable not so much for the incidents of the game as for the unreal atmosphere that pervaded.' The previous day, Germany had invaded Poland, and, for the second time in a generation, a world war appeared inevitable. At 11.00 am the following morning the nation gathered around their wireless sets to hear Prime Minister Neville Chamberlain announce that 'this country is at war with Germany'.

So, Cyril Done's debut goal was scrubbed from the record books. The Football League had closed down for the duration. But Done would score plenty more in wartime football – and play a significant role when the League started up again for 1946-47 and Liverpool won the title.

Done was scoring goals for Bootle Boys' Brigade when Liverpool manager George Kay signed him on amateur forms in 1936. He became a full-time professional a year later. If his first official senior goal was wiped out, there were plenty more 'unofficial' ones to come: in 6 seasons of wartime football – he served in the Army and then as a civilian on essential work – Done scored a remarkable 147 in only 135 matches.

There were hat-tricks galore in the sometimes bizarre scorelines of wartime football, and Done made the papers week after week. After 1 hat-trick, against Manchester City, the *Liverpool Echo* said that his last goal was a header 'that would not have discredited' Dixie Dean. The next week, Done scored 4 goals in a 7-2 win over New Brighton, and the week after that, 3 in a 5-5 draw with the Rakers. Another hat-trick came in a 9-2 win over Burnley, and another as Bury were beaten 7-2, then another in an 8-0 defeat of Crewe Alexandra. He missed playing in a 12-1 thrashing of Southport. Then he suffered appendicitis followed by a broken leg against Manchester City at Anfield in September 1944.

When peacetime football resumed, despite playing in only 17 League matches, Done scored 10 goals including 2 hat-tricks – against Huddersfield Town and Grimsby Town – as the Reds won the title. Done was never going to be the ball-playing type of forward – this he cheerfully admitted – but his ruthless eye for goal, and a terrific shot in his left foot, made him a man to be feared by defenders.

Yet in 1947-48, he was selected only 4 times – and failed to find the net – but made 24 appearances in 1948-49 when he was the Reds' second-highest League scorer, this time with 11 goals. In his last 3 seasons at Anfield, he made only a handful of appearances and, in the 1952 close season, he was transferred to Third Division North Tranmere Rovers for a 4-figure fee. Done had scored 37 goals in 109 peacetime games for the Reds. He scored 75 goals in 97 senior games for Tranmere, and 34 goals in 52 Second Division games for Port Vale. In April 1955, he scored all Vale's goals in a 4-3 win over Liverpool. He ended his playing career with non-League Winsford United and managed Skelmersdale United.

Cyril Done was living in Formby when he died on 24 February 1993, aged 72.

Laurie Hughes

In February 1941, Tranmere Rovers chairman Bob Trueman found himself with a problem. The previous week he had loaned New Brighton a 17-year-old centre-half called Bill Cartwright for a League War Cup-tie at Wrexham. Cartwright was an outstanding success in the Rakers' remarkable 8-5 win at the Racecourse. On the same day, Tranmere beat Chester 9-2 but centre-half Walter Price was injured. Then Tranmere and New Brighton were drawn together in the next round. Price was still injured – and Cartwright was cup-tied. So, Mr Trueman turned to another of his, in his words, 'world-beating youngsters', 16-year-old Laurie Hughes, captain of Tranmere's B team. *The Liverpool Evening Express* columnist 'Pilot' said, 'It is asking a lot of a youngster to step right in for an important cup-tie, but I am certain that Mr Trueman's confidence will not be misplaced.'

Indeed, it was not. Young Cartwright could not prevent his own club from winning 4-3 over 2 legs, and Hughes was on his way to establishing himself. Two years later, he was captaining Tranmere when, in February 1943, Liverpool swooped to sign him on professional forms. Pilot said that the news would come as a bombshell to Tranmere supporters:

> Hughes is one of the outstanding football discoveries of the war, and only last Saturday played a brilliant game against Liverpool at Anfield. Whether Liverpool will eventually make a donation to Tranmere remains to be seen. Hughes and his father asked for the cancellation of the player's amateur registration … . He has now taken the professional ticket with Liverpool who, for months, have held the player in high esteem.

Tranmere were furious. Hughes, who was born in Waterloo on Merseyside in March 1924, had been with them since he joined from Lawrence Road School 4 years earlier. They announced a ban on any Liverpool director being a guest at Prenton Park unless Liverpool were playing there, refused to play their George Mahon Cup match against Liverpool Reserves that weekend, and said that if Liverpool did offer them any compensation for Hughes they would donate it to the Mayor of Birkenhead's War Fund. Bob Trueman said, 'Though no rule has been infringed, we consider that Liverpool's action was unsporting and not what one has the right to expect from a neighbour ... we wish him well, though, and his progress will be watched with kindly interest by the Tranmere club.'

Liverpool's chairman, Richard Martindale, defended their actions saying, 'The Tranmere chairman gave us permission to interview the player. Had he said that he would rather we didn't, then we would have dropped the matter at once.'

Liverpool nursed Hughes through the rest of that season, but in 1943-44 he played in all but 1 game, and he missed only 3 matches in 1944-45. He appeared in 3 of the Reds' 4 FA Cup matches when the competition resumed in 1945-46. When Liverpool won the League championship the following season, Hughes played in 30 of their 42 matches. Injuries meant that he was absent for much of 1948-49 and 1952-53, though. He recovered from a broken toe to play in the 1950 FA Cup final defeat by Arsenal, and that summer won 3 caps in the ill-fated World Cup finals in Brazil during which England lost 1-0 to the USA.

An elegant rather than hard centre-half, Hughes might have won more caps but for the presence of Stoke City's Neil Franklin, who had a similar style. Playing for a World Cup XI against an FA Canadian Touring XI in the 1950 FA Charity Shield match at Stamford Bridge, Hughes was injured and never selected again. He was never quite the same player as injuries caught up with him. That said, he missed only 1 League game in 1956-57 when Liverpool missed promotion to the First Division by only 1 point. He made his final senior appearance for the Reds in a 5-1 defeat by Charlton Athletic at The Valley in September 1957. He had made 326 senior appearances and scored 1 goal. Laurie Hughes died in Liverpool on 9 September 2011, aged 87.

Billy Liddell

One day in 1942, Billy Liddell discovered that airmen at RAF Heaton Park, near Manchester, were not allowed off the base until 4.30 pm on Saturdays. When his application to be released at midday was refused, he climbed over a wall to join up with his Liverpool teammates. Such were the vagaries of the sport during the Second World War, when the young man from Fife should have been starting out on his football career but had to wait until the war was over before it could begin in earnest.

The eldest of 6 children – his father was a miner – Billy Liddell was born at Townhill, near Dunfermline, on 10 January 1922. He played for Lochgelly Violet in the Fife County League. In July 1938, now a Scotland schoolboy international, Liddell signed for Liverpool with Lochgelly Violet receiving a welcome £500. Liddell was assured that he could continue his studies to become a chartered accountant. The family's Presbyterian minister also had to be satisfied that young Billy would not fall into bad company on Merseyside.

In January 1942, the *Daily Record* reported:

> William Liddell is his name, and he is undoubtedly one of the 'big men' of wartime soccer in England … . Liverpool kept him back as long as they could, realising what a player they had got, but soon after the outbreak of war, with all their players in the Territorials, they had to push him into the side. He was then 16 [he was actually almost 18] and has never lost his place since. [There are] not many faults about his play, but [a] feature is the way he beats a back on the inside … . Looks good to me.

Liddell made his Liverpool first-team debut at outside-left in a 7-3 win over Crewe Alexandra on 1 January 1940, and scored with a header from a low Nieuwenhuys cross. Five days later, he netted a hat-trick as Liverpool put another 7 past Manchester City, Frank Swift and all. The *Liverpool Echo* said, 'At 17 years of age this well-built young Dunfermline boy makes an impression as the kind of fellow who will make good in a big way in due course. Moreover, he has the headpiece not to lose his sense of proportion.'

In April 1942, he played for Scotland against England before 70,000 at Hampden Park. The Scots won 5-4 and Liddell marked his wartime international debut with a goal. In December, Liddell, who had been on deferred call-up so that he could continue his accountancy studies, reported to the RAF at Lord's Cricket Ground. If it hadn't been for a navigation course at RAF Bridgnorth – where he suffered a broken leg playing in a station friendly – and 7 months in Canada to complete his qualifications as a navigator, he would have won more than 8 wartime caps. He ended the war bringing back soldiers on leave from Italy.

Demobbed later than most of his teammates, Liddell made his peacetime debut for Liverpool by scoring twice in a 7-4 win over Chelsea at Anfield on 7 September 1946. Eight months later, Liverpool were League champions, and teetotal Billy Liddell declined a sip of champagne from the trophy. In 1950, he played in the FA Cup final defeat by Arsenal. In a way, the result foreshadowed the club's decline and, in 1953-54, the Reds were relegated. That was the only season between 1950 and 1958 that he was not Liverpool's top scorer. No wonder Liverpool were sometimes known as 'Liddellpool'.

Liddell played a handful of games under Bill Shankly before retiring in 1960. Two-footed, he could play on either wing or at centre-forward with equal effect. He scored 229 goals in 536 senior games for Liverpool, won 28 peacetime caps, and he and Stanley Matthews were the only players to appear in both Great Britain teams against the Rest of Europe, in 1947 and 1955.

Billy Liddell, whose life extended well beyond football – he became assistant secretary and bursar at Liverpool University, a justice of the peace, a youth worker and a Sunday School teacher – died on 3 July 2001.

Albert Stubbins

On 6 March 1948, the teams lined up for the second half of the match between Liverpool and Huddersfield Town at Anfield. A whistle blew and the game had been under way for half a minute when the referee, Mr H. T. Wright of Macclesfield, and his 2 linesmen strolled out of the tunnel. It was someone in the crowd who had signalled the restart. Mr Wright dashed on to the pitch and blew his whistle to stop play. Liverpool picked up where they had left off, scored another 2 and won 4-0, with all the goals coming from Albert Stubbins. By the end of the season, Stubbins was Liverpool's leading League scorer with 24 goals, the same figure that the previous season had seen him joint leading scorer, with Jack Balmer, as the Reds won the first League championship of the post-war era.

Born in Wallsend on 17 July 1919, but brought up in the USA before returning England in 1930, Stubbins trained as a draughtsman and played as an amateur for Sunderland before joining Newcastle United in April 1937. The war interrupted his Football League career but in wartime football itself, he scored an astonishing number of goals – 245 in only 199 matches – and won an England cap. When peace was restored, he was hot property.

In September 1946, Stubbins was surprisingly placed on the transfer list at his own request after Newcastle signed George Stobbart, another goalscorer who had made his name in wartime football, with Middlesbrough. *The Shields Daily News* said Newcastle were 'flooded with offers' for Stubbins, who had been disappointed with his form and thought that a change of club would do him good. The *Liverpool Echo* felt that it would be easier to list those clubs not interested in Stubbins and reported that on Liverpool's behalf 'George Kay dashed off post-haste to Newcastle after last night's game [a 5-0 thumping for Liverpool at Old Trafford] and chairman Bill McConnell followed this morning.

Theo Kelly will conduct the negotiations for Everton.' On Friday, 13 September, the *Daily Herald* reported that it had come down to a battle between Liverpool and Everton who had each offered Newcastle £13,000. The Merseyside clubs decided to leave it to Stubbins, who had gone to a news cinema. Someone went to fetch him and he decided on Anfield rather than Goodison. The following day, a wet and dreary afternoon at Burnden Park, Stubbins scored on his Liverpool debut, the Reds' second goal in a late 3-1 win over Bolton Wanderers. By the end of the season, Liverpool were champions and Stubbins had added 4 FA Cup goals – including a hat-trick against Birmingham City – to his League tally.

In 1948-49, however, he entered into a dispute with Liverpool. He did not turn up for pre-season training, and demanded a transfer but his request was refused. The *Daily Mirror* reported that 'Red-haired Albert Stubbins packed his belongings and moved back to his native Newcastle. "My chief aim at the moment is to take a small business on Tyneside," he said. "What happens so far as football is concerned is in the lap of the gods."' Clubs, though, held all the cards in those days and eventually Stubbins – who was now writing a regular column in the *Liverpool Echo* – re-signed. But now injuries began to dog him. That season he made only 15 League appearances (but still scored 6 goals). Although Stubbins remained at Anfield for a further 4 seasons, he was never the same player, and on 3 January 1953, he played his last match for Liverpool, a 3-1 defeat at Stoke. At the age of 34, he retired. He had scored 83 goals in 180 League and FA Cup matches for the Reds. He played for and briefly managed non-League Ashington, coached in New York for a short while, and became a full-time sports journalist. Albert Stubbins, whose image, thanks to Liverpool supporter Paul McCartney, appeared on the front over of The Beatles' album *Sgt. Pepper's Lonely Hearts Club Band*, died in Cullercoats on Tyneside on 28 December 2002, aged 83.

Bill Jones

For over a million people there was only 1 place to be on Saturday, 31 August 1946 – at a Football League ground. Unusually for the first day of the football season, the weather was cloudy and overcast and the forecast was rain. The previous week had seen gale-force winds and torrential downpours, rivers swollen, roads blocked by fallen trees. Still, in Britain, the days when football matches were interrupted by air raids, and teams made up their numbers by borrowing from their opponents, or even from the crowd, were over. Now there was a return to the old ways of football.

The fixtures were a replica of those on the opening day of the 1939-40 season, which meant that 28,000 fans made their way to Bramall Lane, where Liverpool, fresh from their trip to North America to stock up on calories, were Sheffield United's visitors. Thanks to a last-minute goal from Len Carney, the Reds began the post-war era in victorious fashion. It was Carney's first taste of proper League football, as it was for many players that day. One of them was a Derbyshire-born 25-year-old utility man called Bill Jones, who had been at Anfield since September 1938 when he joined Liverpool from Hayfield St Matthew's of the Stockport Sunday School League. He made his first senior appearance at inside-right against Sheffield United in the League War Cup at Anfield in February 1942, and marked it with a goal.

During the war, Jones also guested for York City, Leeds United and Reading, and found time to win the Military Medal while serving with the King's Regiment during the Allied crossing of the Rhine in 1945.

Back in Liverpool, he went straight into the Reds' team for that first post-war season. A week after his debut, he scored twice as the Reds beat Chelsea 7-4 at Anfield, and he proved so versatile that, before the season's end, he had appeared in no less than 6 different positions: centre-forward, inside-left, left-half, centre-half, right-half and left-back. Writing in the *Liverpool Echo* in January 1947, Albert Stubbins said:

> The number of positions in which certain players appear during their soccer careers is remarkable, and at Liverpool, Bill Jones has proved to be one of the best utility men in football. It is strange to think that in my first game with Liverpool, at Bolton, Bill played a sparkling game at inside-forward, and after seeing his displays at wing-half and full-back recently, Anfield supporters would probably feel no surprise to see him play well in any position.

The same month, previewing a First Division visit from Grimsby Town, the *Liverpool Echo*'s columnist 'Ranger' said, 'The absence of Hughes is not the blow to Liverpool it might have been. They have a talented and skilful player in Bill Jones to fill the breach.' Jones was, according to the *Echo*, 'a string tackler, splendid header of the ball, and always seeking to make intelligent use of clearances as a means of initiating a counter-attack.'

In 1950, Jones was a member of the first Liverpool team to play at Wembley, although the FA Cup final against Arsenal ended in disappointment. In May that year, he also won his first England cap, a friendly against Portugal in Lisbon, and 4 days later he was capped again, in another friendly, this time against Belgium in Brussels. Both times he played at centre-half and he was selected in the provisional squad for that summer's World Cup in Brazil but did not make the final cut.

After 278 League and FA Cup appearances, and 17 goals, for Liverpool, Jones left the Reds in 1954, at the end of the relegation season, to join Ellesmere Port Town as player-manager. He once confided that had Liverpool not signed him from a Derbyshire junior club, he might have tried to make his living as a golf professional, and he was also a talented cricketer.

Bill Jones died in a Chester hospital on 26 December 2010. He was 89. His grandson is Rob Jones, the Liverpool and England defender.

Ray Lambert

On 2 September 1939, Ray Lambert was playing for Liverpool Reserves against Preston North End Reserves in a Central League match at Deepdale when he decided to pass back to his goalkeeper, Eric Mansley. It went down as an own-goal against the right-back. The following day, Britain declared war on Germany, and 17-year-old Lambert would have to wait 6 years for a chance in the Football League. Two months later, though, he did make his first-team debut, in a War League match at Wrexham. The *Liverpool Echo* described him as 'rather leggy' but felt that 'when he has filled out and added another couple of years on his shoulders and another couple of stone to his weight he should make a first-class centre-half.'

Lambert was then the youngest player ever signed by a Football League club. He was 13 years and 189 days old when George Kay took him on in September 1936. Born in Flint in 1922, Lambert was a bright star, playing at centre-half for Wales Schoolboys. On his 17th birthday, he became a full-time professional on £5 a week, and an extra £1 when he played in the first team.

After his senior debut at Wrexham, he fractured an ankle playing against Blackpool Reserves, and so missed much of the rest of that season, but in 1940-41, he was ever-present and earning rave reviews. In September 1942, Lambert was called up for military service, but whenever he was available after that he got a game for Liverpool and also guested for Reading, although a ruptured muscle when he played for Wales in their 8-3 defeat by England at Wembley in September 1943 also sidelined him for several months.

The war at an end, Lambert made his long-awaited official debut for the Reds in the 1945-46 FA Cup, at Sealand Road, Chester, where Billy Liddell and Bob Paisley were also making their first peacetime appearances that afternoon. Lambert's Football League debut came the following season, in a 3-1 win against Bolton Wanderers at Burnden Park, on the same day that Albert Stubbins played his first game for Liverpool. Once in the side, Lambert was rarely out of it again as the Reds won the title in a thrilling finish to a long season. The *Liverpool Echo* said that he had enjoyed a great season: 'He is one of the deadliest tacklers in the game with exceptional powers of recovery.'

For the next few seasons, Lambert continued his run in the side, either at right or left-back, becoming 1 of the most reliable defenders in the club's history. He was also capped again by Wales, this time officially – wartime caps did not count, despite the fact that teams fielded by the home nations were often some of the strongest ever – with the first of his 5 caps coming in a 3-1 win over Scotland at Wrexham in October 1946. His Liverpool teammate Billy Liddell was in the opposing line-up.

That month, along with Liddell and goalkeeper Cyril Sidlow, Lambert was still waiting to be demobbed, and such was a footballer's life in those early post-war days that travelling back to his unit after playing for Liverpool in their 6-1 win at Grimsby Town, he arrived at York early on the Sunday morning to discover that he had to wait hours for his connection. A friendly railway official tried to arrange for Lambert to continue his journey north on a goods train bound for Darlington, but was unsuccessful.

In December 1947, Lambert might have been on his way out of Anfield, when Liverpool offered him or Phil Taylor plus a fee for Newcastle United's inside-forward Roy Bentley. In the end, Bentley went to Chelsea.

Ray Lambert retired in 1956, by which time Liverpool were a Second Division club. He had made 341 senior appearances for Liverpool and scored 2 goals. He then ran a newsagent's business on Deeside. After he died on 22 October 2009, aged 87, his football trophies were found in a bag at the back of a wardrobe.

Don Welsh

When Liverpool were winning the first post-war Football League championship, Don Welsh was on his way to winning the FA Cup. The previous season, Welsh had played in the final, for Charlton Athletic in their 4-1 extra-time defeat by Derby County. Twelve months later, he was back at Wembley, this time on the winning side as Charlton – the club he had captained from the Third Division South to the First Division before the war – beat Burnley 1-0. After the game, Welsh demanded £2 10s a head from photographers wishing to take a picture of the winning team.

Winning 3 England caps before the war, he scored 50 goals in 216 League and FA Cup appearances for Charlton as well as 100 goals in 118 wartime games. Liverpool supporters remembered him for his 6 goals in a 12-1 win over Southport in December 1944, when he guested for the Reds. After he retired from playing, Manchester-born Welsh took the job of Brighton and Hove Albion manager in November 1947, but he could not prevent the club from finishing bottom of the Third Division South in his first season.

Brighton's fortunes improved, but it was still a surprise to some when, in March 1951, Welsh was Liverpool's choice to take over from George Kay, who had retired because of ill-health. However, Ranger, the *Liverpool Echo* columnist, had no such reservations. He felt that the Liverpool board had made an excellent choice because Welsh was among the top flight of post-war managers who were bringing a new outlook and fresh ideas to the game. At only 40 years of age, said Ranger, Welsh was still young enough to take part in practice games in order to demonstrate his theories, and that, combined with his own impressive playing record, would obviously command respect from the players in his charge. He had proved to be a popular wartime guest at Anfield, when his 40 games yielded 43 goals, and when Matt Busby had taken over as manager of Manchester United in 1945, Welsh's name had been mentioned in connection with a coaching job at Liverpool, but, at the time, he felt that he had a few more years left as a player.

At Brighton, Welsh had introduced some novel ideas including directing practice matches over the public-address system, installing 'shooting boxes' so that the ball came back at various heights and angles, thus honing players' skills in quick thinking and instant mastery. Ranger also felt that Welsh possessed a pleasing personality and a cheery outlook that endeared him to those under his care. And, besides that double hat-trick against Southport, he also once scored 3 in the last 8 minutes of a game against Everton. That was always going to give him a special place in Liverpool hearts.

Alas, at Anfield, Welsh struggled to make an impression as manager. He introduced Alan A'Court, Ronnie Moran and Louis Bimpson, but the £12,000 he spent on Wolves' Sammy Smyth was perhaps too much, for even though Smyth scored 20 goals for Liverpool, his best days were, undeniably, behind him and he made only 45 appearances. Welsh continued to spend, but in 1953-54, the Reds lost the First Division place they had enjoyed since 1905. Back in the Second Division, Liverpool then suffered the biggest defeat in their history, a humiliating 9-1 thrashing at Birmingham City in December 1954. Gradually, the skies over Anfield brightened again, and in 1955-56, Welsh took the Reds to third place. It was close but not close enough, and in May 1956, the Liverpool board accepted his resignation. The *Liverpool Echo* said it understood that the manager had not seen eye-to-eye with the directors 'for quite some time'. It was a sad but inevitable parting.

Welsh managed Bournemouth from 1958 to 1961, coached Wycombe Wanderers and returned to Charlton as a member of their administrative staff. He also ran a pub in Devon and worked in local government as a coach and teacher in north London. Don Welsh died in Stevenage on 2 February 1990, aged 78.

Phil Taylor

After Don Welsh's resignation as Liverpool manager in May 1956, the initial feeling was that, for the time being, a directorial sub-committee would look after playing matters. No need to rush into these things. Across Stanley Park, Everton had chosen that approach, albeit with a spectacular lack of success, after sacking Cliff Britton the previous February. At Anfield, that initial idea was quickly jettisoned, and the names of Billy Liddell or Phil Taylor were suggested as Welsh's replacement.

Taylor, already the Reds' chief coach, was the stronger candidate, and was given the job. It seemed a somewhat reluctant choice, though. His title was to be 'liaison official', a link between players and training staff, and the directors. A few days later, the board decided that Taylor would be known as 'acting team manager'. By the summer of 1957, the *Liverpool Echo* was calling him the 'manager'. Whatever, Taylor would go down in history as the only Liverpool boss never to manage the club in the First Division.

His playing pedigree was entirely different. His association with Liverpool went back to March 1936, when he joined the Reds from his hometown club, Bristol Rovers, for £5,000. In those early days, he was a centre-forward and he scored on his League debut for Liverpool – a 90th-minute equaliser against Derby County at the Baseball Ground in March 1936, 'a beautiful low ball, well-placed and a golden goal ... his crowning triumph in a smart day's work, and it is good to know that he is a likeable fellow who will not be affected by success in a new city,' according to the *Liverpool Echo*.

In fact, it was the first of only 34 goals Taylor would score in 345 League and FA Cup appearances for Liverpool because he switched from the forward line to become a stylish wing-half who eventually took over from Matt Busby. Busby's playing career ended during the

Second World War whereas the younger Taylor – he was 22 when war was declared; Busby was 30 – had some playing years left in him when peace was restored.

In the autumn of 1947, a few months after celebrating Liverpool's First Division title triumph, Taylor was capped 3 times for England, against Wales, Northern Ireland and Sweden, and in 1949-50 he took over the Liverpool captaincy from Jack Balmer, and thus led Liverpool out for the FA Cup final against Arsenal. He made his last appearance for the Reds in a 5-2 defeat by West Brom at The Hawthorns in March 1954, towards the end of a season in which Liverpool finished rock bottom of the First Division. He joined the coaching staff under Don Welsh, and, when Welsh decided that he had had enough of Liverpool, and the club's directors decided that they had had enough of Welsh, it was Taylor who stepped into what was then one of the most difficult jobs in football.

In his first season, Liverpool finished third, behind promoted Leicester City and Nottingham Forest, and then fourth and fourth again. It was good, but far from good enough. There was also a shock FA Cup defeat at the hands of non-League Worcester City. On 17 November 1959, Taylor handed in his resignation and the board accepted it. It was said to be an amicable parting. Again, Billy Liddell's name was mentioned as player-manager. There was speculation that Scottish coach Reuben Bennett would be temporarily promoted until a permanent replacement was appointed. Bob Paisley, the former player who was now the club's head trainer, was also considered, by the press and the supporters at least.

In the meantime, Phil Taylor was left to reflect on his 3 years as manager. In 2003, he recalled, 'Don Welsh and myself had to present our teams to full board meetings, often involving 8 or 9 directors ... I can remember times when the side that ran out was not really the one I wanted to play.'

Phil Taylor was thought to be the oldest surviving England footballer before he died on 1 December 2012, aged 95.

Louis Bimpson

Born in Rainford, Lancashire, on 14 May 1929, Louis Bimpson joined Liverpool in January 1953. Despite making relatively few appearances, there were some real highlights, not least in 1953-54 when he was joint top scorer, with Sam Smyth who also had 13 goals. That relegation season was an odd one, for sure. Liverpool lost 6-0 at Charlton Athletic, and in consecutive games in December – at Fratton Park, Old Trafford and The Hawthorns – shipped 5 goals each time. Yet they beat Aston Villa 6-1 at Anfield in October – Bimpson did not score that day and then missed 3 games because of blood poisoning. He reported sick as the players boarded a train for Huddersfield and someone had to get Alan A'Court out of bed to take his place. There were other big scores when he was involved. In a 4-4 draw with Manchester United at Anfield in the second game of the season, for instance, Bimpson scored twice; and when, a month later, Burnley were beaten 4-0, also at Anfield, Bimpson scored all the goals in the first half.

On 6 November 1953, on the eve of the visit of Manchester City, the *Liverpool Echo* said, 'The return of Bimpson will be welcomed by Liverpool followers. The former Burscough player is a speedy and determined raider, often making openings by sheer persistence where none seem to exist.' The match ended 2-2 and to underline the point, the *Echo* reported, 'Bimpson, back after missing 3 games, got 2 nasty knocks on the head which left him dazed and very largely accounted for his loss of speed. Without it, he was no great danger. Yet his persistence brought Liverpool's opening goal.'

After that personal peak in an otherwise awful season for Liverpool, Bimpson never played more than half the games in any 1 season. Yet he was always among the goals. In 1958-59, he played in only 15 Second Division matches but still scored 11 times. He might have played in more games but for injuries – he underwent an operation on an instep – and a bout of 'flu. At the start of the season, the *Liverpool Echo* said, 'Whether Bimpson is or is not a better centre-forward than Liddell is now of academic interest. The point is that the side seem to play better for his presence in the attack.'

It was a rare moment of praise. Reporting on the 2-1 defeat at Lincoln City in March 1959, the newspaper said, 'Bimpson's heading, apart from his goal, was disappointing in the extreme.' And when Liverpool beat Plymouth Argyle 4-1 at Anfield in September 1959: 'Bimpson's display stressed the importance more than ever for an immediate centre-forward signing. Louis couldn't do much right.'

On 19 November 1959, Blackburn Rovers' manager Dally Duncan signed Bimpson from Liverpool for £5,500. Although not a regular first-teamer – he often seemed to be fighting for a place wherever he went – Bimpson played in every round of Blackburn Rovers' march to the 1960 FA Cup final. That season he scored twice in 16 First Division matches, but missed only 2 out of 9 FA Cup ties – Blackburn were involved in no less than 3 replays – and scored 3 goals on the way to Wembley. Overall, he made only 22 League appearances in his 3 seasons at Ewood Park, where he was used mostly as an outside-right – and, at 6ft tall, a burly one at that – and the story had not been much different during his career with Liverpool – only 100 League and FA Cup appearances in his 8 seasons at Anfield, although 40 goals which was a good strike rate. The 1960-61 season saw Bimpson make only 6 League appearances for Blackburn, and in February 1961 he was transferred to Bournemouth, then managed by Don Welsh. Six months later he moved to Chester. There was perhaps a sweet moment when he helped Chester beat Blackburn in the 1961-62 Football League Cup semi-final. In July 1963, he moved to Wigan Athletic, who were then in the Cheshire League, before ending his career back at Burscough.

Ronnie Moran

On 22 November 1952, Liverpool lost 3-2 at Derby to a team destined to finish at the foot of the First Division that season. Liverpool themselves were going through a difficult patch and would finish only 2 points ahead of Stoke City, the club that would accompany Derby into the Second Division. But then these were different times: Chelsea and Manchester City would also narrowly miss relegation in coronation year.

The Reds had injury worries that November. Which meant a first-team debut for 18-year-old left-back Ronnie Moran. The youngster had a shaky start at Derby, but the *Liverpool Echo* said, 'Once Moran had settled down, he held his own quite well and his second-half positional play and tackling showed good promise.'

It was the first of 379 senior appearances that Ronnie Moran would make for Liverpool, a club he would serve as player, captain, coach for both reserve and first teams, physiotherapist and caretaker manager in an Anfield career that spanned half a century and no less than 9 managers. He also scored 16 goals, mostly from the penalty spot, although he missed a few, including 1 in February 1964, in the 80th minute of an FA Cup quarter-final against Swansea Town who won 2-1.

He was a local lad, born in Crosby on 28 February 1934, and had just started his apprenticeship as an electrician when he joined Liverpool on amateur forms in 1949. Three years later, just before his 18th birthday, he signed as a full-time professional on £14 a week in the season and £11 a week in the summer. The story goes that the postman who delivered to Liverpool's chairman, Councillor Samuel Williams, recommended him to the club. One week later, an Everton scout approached Moran, only to discover that he was too late.

Moran made 11 League appearances in 1952-53, but played only once when the Reds were relegated the following season. It was in the Second Division that he finally established himself as a first-team regular, and between 1955-56 and 1959-60 he missed only 5 League matches out of a possible 210. Injuries restricted his appearances in the next 2 seasons – he played only 16 times when the Reds won the Second Division title in 1961-62 – but then he regained his place and when Liverpool won the First Division in 1963-64 he played 35 times. He missed the following season's FA Cup final, however; by then Gerry Byrne was well established.

Moran played his final match for Liverpool on 20 March 1965, in a 3-2 win over Fulham at Anfield. Two days later he was named in the party of 15 players that travelled to Rotterdam to play 1. FC Cologne in a European Cup quarter-final second replay. He watched from the sidelines as the Reds went through on the toss of a coin.

His Liverpool playing career was over but he did not leave Anfield. Bill Shankly asked him if he would like to join the backroom staff. Moran told *LFChistory.net*:

> I went off and discussed it with my wife. We are both from Liverpool and didn't want to leave, and the next day I told Bill, 'Yes'. We never really discussed a specific role. I guess Shanks and Bob [Paisley] had seen me shouting and talking a lot when I was playing and liked what they'd seen. They just let me get on with it.

The man Tommy Smith once said 'could moan for England' became a vital part of the famous Anfield bootroom staff. Twice he stepped up to manage the team, first after Kenny Dalglish resigned, and then when Graeme Souness went into hospital for heart surgery. After Souness returned, he chose the team for the 1992 FA Cup final together with Moran, and it was Moran who led the team out at Wembley. Long after his retirement he was still a regular visitor to Liverpool's training ground

Ronnie Moran died on 22 March 2017, aged 83. The title of a book about his career had been published 2 weeks earlier. It was called simply *Mr Liverpool*.

Alan A'Court

In the 1951-52 season, Football League scouts were alerted to a 17-year-old outside-left playing for Prescot Cables in the Lancashire Combination. Alan A'Court was a schoolboy star with Prescot Grammar School and the Liverpool FA youth teams. Now Liverpool, Everton, Bolton Wanderers and Wolves were taking an interest. A'Court chose Anfield. In August 1952, he signed for the Reds on amateur forms. A month later he was a professional. It was the start of an outstanding career.

A'Court did not have long to wait for his chance. On 7 February 1953, he made his debut at a snowy Ayresome Park where Liverpool beat Middlesbrough 3-2. The *Liverpool Echo* reported, 'A'Court's first pass saw him slip past Bilcliff cleverly and send over a strong centre from the touchline which led to a melee in front of the Middlesbrough goal but nothing more … A'Court was most tenacious in his work whenever he got the ball.'

He was 1 of 3 debutants that day, joining the tall South African centre-half Hugh Gerhardi, and right-half Roy Saunders, a former Hull City amateur, who were also taking their first steps in senior football. Their futures were mixed. Gerhardi played only 6 times before returning to South Africa. Saunders made 144 appearances before signing for Swansea Town in 1959, his path at Anfield blocked for much of the time by the presence of Phil Taylor and Bob Paisley.

A'Court, however, went from strength to strength. He played 12 times in his first season, had 16 games when Liverpool were relegated in 1953-54, but then in the Second Division was rarely out of the team. In fact, over the next 8 seasons he missed only 32 League games out of a possible 336. When Liverpool won the Second Division title in 1961-62, he played in every game. He possessed a fierce shot that altogether brought him 63 League and FA Cup goals, and in total played in 382 League,

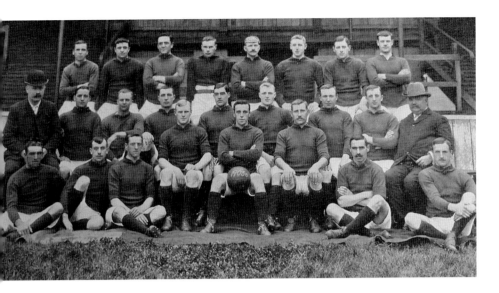

Liverpool pictured in 1905-06. The newly promoted Reds won the First Division title that season. (Author's collection)

Jack Cox, a fast goal-scoring winger who was capped for England and won 2 League championship medals with Liverpool in the 1900s. (Author's collection)

Scotland's Ned Doig, the first in a long line of Liverpool's international goalkeepers. He moved to Anfield from Sunderland in 1904. (Author's collection)

Sam Raybould, whose 31 League goals in 1902-03 stood as a Liverpool club record until Gordon Hodgson broke it 29 years later. (Author's collection)

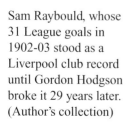

Full-back Billy Dunlop enjoyed 15 years at Anfield before the First World War, making 358 appearances. (Author's collection)

Anfield stadium, pictured in 1908 when Liverpool sat mid-table in the First Division. (Liverpool Record Office, Liverpool Libraries)

LIVERPOOL F.C.

Liverpool's playing staff at the start of 1913-14, a season in which they finished 16th in the First Division and were FA Cup runners-up. (Author's collection)

South African Gordon Hodgson scored 240 goals in 378 appearances for Liverpool between the wars. (PA Images)

Tom Cooper captained Liverpool and England. He lost his life in a wartime motoring accident while serving in the Army. (Author's collection)

Jack Balmer scored hat-tricks in 3 consecutive matches as Liverpool won the first post-war League championship. (PA Images)

Phil Taylor led Liverpool to the 1950 FA Cup and later managed the Reds. (PA Images)

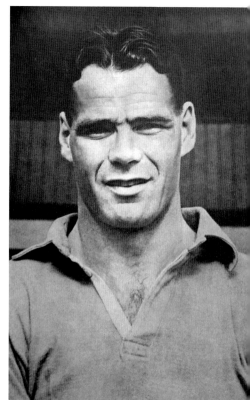

Billy Liddell, whose 229 goals in 536 appearances between 1945-46 and 1960-61 made him a Liverpool legend. (Author's collection)

A rare photograph of Albert
Stubbins, English football's top
goalscorer in wartime football,
with his eyes not on the ball.
(Author's collection)

Dave Hickson heads goalwards
against Derby County at Anfield in
October 1960. Roger Hunt looks on.
It was Bill Shankly's first full season
in charge. (Author's collection)

Roger Hunt scored 41 goals in Liverpool's 1961-62 promotion season. By the end of his career he had 285 goals for Liverpool and a host of medals including the 1966 World Cup. (PA Images)

Ron Yeats and Gordon Milne hold up the FA Cup after Liverpool beat Leeds United at Wembley in 1965. (PA Images)

Bill Shankly pictured with new signing Kevin Keegan at Anfield in May 1971.
(PA Images)

A supporter wants to shake hands with Brian Hall after Liverpool lost at the
Baseball Ground in May 1972. Liverpool failed to win at Arsenal in their last game
and the title went to Derby. (Author's collection)

Liverpool had just drawn with Leicester City at Anfield in April 1973 and Tommy Smith was not letting go of the Football League Championship trophy. (PA Images)

Bill Shankly acknowledges the Anfield crowd after the Reds won the Football League Championship in 1973. (PA Images)

Jimmy Case and Ray Kennedy celebrate with the European Cup after Liverpool's victory over Borussia Mönchengladbach in 1977. (PA Images)

Bob Paisley with new signing Kenny Dalglish in August 1977. (PA Images)

Wise heads – from left to right, Ronnie Moran, Bob Paisley and Joe Fagan in the Anfield dugout, November 1979. (PA Images)

Joe Fagan, the first English club manager to win 3 major trophies in a single season. (PA Images)

Alan Kennedy fires home the winning penalty in the 1984 European Cup final against AS Roma in Rome. (PA Images)

Player-manager Kenny Dalglish celebrates what proved to the title-winning goal against Chelsea at Stamford Bridge in May 1986. (PA Images)

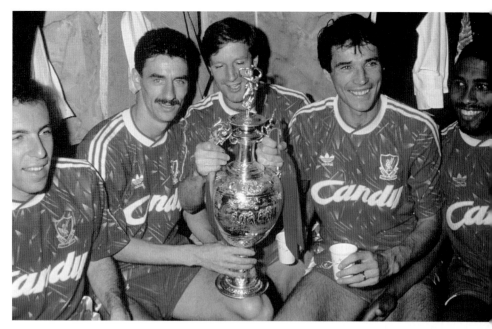

From left to right, Ronny Rosenthal, Ian Rush, Ronnie Whelan, Alan Hansen and John Barnes with the League Championship trophy after Liverpool beat Derby County at Anfield in May 1990. (PA Images)

Roy Evans forces a smile as Gérard Houllier is unveiled as his new co-manager. (PA Images)

Ecstatic fans surround Liverpool's bus as the team arrives back at Anfield after the incredible 2005 Champions League final in Istanbul. (PA Images)

Virgil van Dijk congratulates Mo Salah on scoring Liverpool's third goal against Red Star Belgrade in the Champions League group game at Anfield in October 2018. (PA Images)

Back home – Jürgen Klopp and Jordan Henderson bring back the Champions League trophy in 2019. (PA Images)

Mo Salah smiles as the trophy becomes part of the team's luggage. (PA Images)

FA Cup and League Cup matches for the Reds. His final game – in fact his only game in 2 seasons – came, surprisingly, in his only appearance in European competition, against KR Reykjavik on 14 September 1964 in the preliminary round of the European Cup. The *Liverpool Echo* said, 'A'Court, as a deputy left wing in place of the injured Wallace and Thompson, must have covered every inch of the pitch with hardly a challenge until he neared the Reykjavik defensive wall.' Liverpool won 6-1 to take the tie 11-1 on aggregate.

In October 1964, A'Court moved to Tranmere Rovers for £4,500, looking back on a Liverpool career that brought him only that Second Division winners' medal. When Liverpool were back in the First Division he missed half the season through injury, and then lost his place to Peter Thompson, who retained the number-11 shirt for the entire League championship-winning season of 1963-64.

Even as a Second Division player he had won full England honours, making a scoring debut against Northern Ireland in November 1957, although the Irish won 3-2 at Wembley. He won 5 caps altogether, 3 of them coming in the 1958 World Cup finals in Sweden, against Brazil, Austria and the USSR, when he came into the side after Preston's Tom Finney was injured and thus faced the unenviable task of standing in for, perhaps, the 1 player of true world class in the England squad. A'Court's last appearance was in the 2-2 draw with Wales at Villa Park in November 1958. His international recognition had attracted the attention of several First Division clubs, including Arsenal who were said to have bid £12,000 to take him to Highbury, but A'Court and Liverpool were happy together.

After leaving Tranmere – for whom he had made 50 appearances and scored 11 goals – in 1966, he moved to Norwich City as player-coach, and then worked as assistant manager at both Chester and Crewe Alexandra, Stoke City's coach and, briefly, caretaker manager. He also had coaching jobs in Zambia and New Zealand.

Alan A'Court died in Nantwich on 15 December 2009, aged 75.

Jimmy Melia

When Liverpool beat Nottingham Forest 5-2 at Anfield just before Christmas 1955, it was their eighth home win of the season, further cementing their promotion challenge. For 18-year-old Jimmy Melia it was an especially memorable day. It was his first-team debut and he marked it with a goal, a 48th-minute close-range shot that might have won more column inches had it not been overshadowed by a hat-trick from the evergreen Billy Liddell.

Melia had long been on Liverpool's radar. A local boy, he joined the Reds straight from St Anthony's School on Scotland Road, signed professional forms on his 17th birthday – 1 November 1954 – and added England youth international caps to those he had won as a schoolboy. After a handful of reserve-team matches, Don Welsh gave him his chance at inside-right.

Liverpool did not go up that season, and Melia played only 3 more times, but in 1956-57 he made 26 appearances and scored 6 goals as the Reds again missed promotion by a whisker. After that, Melia was a regular, and when promotion was eventually won, in 1961-62, he never missed a game and weighed in with 12 goals. By now Welsh had gone, and so had his successor, Phil Taylor, and it was Bill Shankly who took Liverpool back into the top flight, 8 points ahead of runners-up Leyton Orient.

Shankly liked Melia and included him in his plans to reshape the team. The First Division did not overawe the player. He missed only 3 games in 1962-63 as the Reds settled in, but when the League championship was won in 1963-64, after playing 24 times he was sold to Wolves for £55,000. Melia's last appearance was not as happy as his debut had been: Liverpool lost 3-1 at Goodison Park, and Melia came in for criticism from some supporters. That was on 8 February 1964. One month later he was on his way to Molineux. He had made 287 senior appearances for Liverpool and scored 78 goals for the Reds.

Melia's transfer came as a surprise to many. The negotiations were done in secrecy because, had it been known that he was available, then there would have been at least half-a-dozen clubs interested. After all, he might have been dropped from the Liverpool team but he was now a full England international, capped for the first time against Scotland at Wembley in April 1963 – the Scots won 2-1 – with a second and final cap coming 2 months later, in an 8-1 win over Switzerland in Basel.

Writing in the *Liverpool Echo*, Leslie Edwards said, 'As his invariable champion I am sorry to see him go. There will be many others sorry, too, but clearly Liverpool would not want to stand in the way of a player for whom no place could be found in the side.'

Wolves manager, Stan Cullis, told reporters, 'We have always admired Jimmy's play. He has always done unusually well against us. We think he will suit our style and we are glad to have such a good club man.'

In fact, Melia spent only a few months with Wolves. He never settled there and by December was on his way to Southampton, for £30,000. Cullis had been sacked and the new manager at Molineux, Andy Beattie, was happy to let him go. Although initially reluctant to move further south still, Melia had a much happier time at The Dell. He helped them into the First Division and was ever-present in the Saints' first season in the top flight, his experience invaluable in a successful battle against an immediate return to the Second Division. After 4 years and 152 games for Southampton, Melia moved to Aldershot as player-manager before finishing his playing career with Crewe Alexandra whom he also managed. As a rather flamboyant manager of Brighton he took the Seagulls to the 1983 FA Cup final. There followed a spell as Southport's manager, then various jobs including managing CF Os Belenense in Portugal, and Stockport County, and scouting and coaching in the Middle East and the USA.

Roger Hunt

In July 1959, Roger Hunt, then an amateur with Liverpool after playing with Glazebury Croft and Stockton Heath, was released from his National Service and returned to his Warrington home. The previous season, he had turned out for Devizes Town while completing his Army training in Wiltshire, during which time he played for an FA Amateur XI against London University, the Young Amateurs of the West against Bristol City, and for the Possibles against the Probables in an FA Olympic trial in Birmingham. Back on Merseyside, and free from military service, he was signed as a professional – and a great Liverpool career got under way.

It did not take Lancashire-born Hunt, by now 21, long to make his mark. In September 1959, he scored on his first-team debut. He had come in for Billy Liddell, who was rested after playing in 4 matches in 11 days. Jimmy Melia opened the scoring in a Second Division match against Scunthorpe United at Anfield. Liverpool won 2-0 on that Wednesday evening, and in the *Liverpool Echo*, Michael Charters wrote, 'it was not until newcomer Hunt, at centre-forward, hit a well-taken second goal in the 64th minute that Liverpool could say the game was theirs … . For his goal alone Hunt did more than others to clinch victory and on that reckoning his debut was not without merit.'

Hunt was 1 of the players who survived the clear-out after Bill Shankly replaced Phil Taylor as manager in November 1959, and how he thrived. He rarely missed a game as the Reds came so near to getting back into the First Division, and when promotion was finally won, in 1961-62, he missed only 1 game, scoring 41 goals in his 41 League appearances, including hat-tricks against Leeds United, Walsall, Swansea Town, Bury and Middlesbrough. When Liverpool won the First Division in 1963-64, and in 1965-66, Hunt was again the Reds' leading scorer each season with 31 goals and 30 goals respectively. In between those 2 triumphs, he also helped Liverpool win the FA Cup for the first time when they beat Leeds United 2-1 at Wembley with Hunt and Ian St John both scoring in extra-time. The following year, Hunt scored Liverpool's goal when they lost 2-1 after extra-time to Borussia Dortmund in the European Cup-winners' Cup final at Hampden Park.

And, of course, there was the not inconsiderable matter of the 1966 World Cup final. He played in all 6 matches and was hat-trick hero Geoff Hurst's strike partner in the final. When it comes to that controversial was-it-over-the-line? goal against West Germany, Hurst always points out that Hunt, had he any doubt, could have stuck it away but instead wheeled away in celebration because he could see the ball had crossed the line. Altogether Hunt won 34 caps and scored 18 goals for his country, included 1 on his debut, against Austria in April 1962.

In all matches – 489 with only 5 as a substitute – Roger Hunt scored 285 goals for Liverpool, which would stand as a record until Ian Rush broke it, although Hunt still holds the record for the most League goals, 245.

In December 1969, he was transferred to Bolton Wanderers. He told the *Daily Mirror*, 'After playing for Liverpool for so long it would be a big wrench to leave them but I recognise that that day must come.' Hunt played for Bolton in the Second and Third Divisions before retiring in the close season of 1972. On 11 April that year, a remarkable attendance of 55,214 turned out on a rainy evening at Anfield for 'Sir Roger' Hunt's testimonial match between the 1965 FA Cup-winning team and an International XI, most of whom were from the 1966 World Cup winners. Liverpool won 8-6 with the help of an own-goal from Martin Peters.

After football, Hunt worked in the family haulage business. Along with those who had not already been similarly honoured for their World Cup win – Ray Wilson, Alan Ball, George Cohen and Nobby Stiles – in 2000, Hunt was awarded the MBE.

Gerry Byrne

Full-back Gerry Byrne could hardly have had a worse start to his Liverpool first-team career. He arrived at Anfield as a 15 year old, spotted playing in a match in Dublin for Liverpool Catholic Schoolboys – he was born in Liverpool on 29 August 1938 – and he became a professional in August 1955. He had to wait another 2 years for his debut, and what an afternoon it was. On 28 September 1957, Liverpool lost 5-1 at Charlton Athletic, – where Byrne put through his own goal, prodding a back pass beyond the reach of Tommy Younger.

The match nearly did not take place. Along with most League clubs, Liverpool were struggling to raise a full team because of the 'flu epidemic that was killing thousands of people worldwide. The Reds considered asking for a postponement but eventually managed to raise a team in which Byrne was 1 of several reserves to step in. For a top-of-the table clash it was an unusually one-sided affair, and one for debutant Gerry Byrne to quickly forget.

In his first 5 years as a professional, he was rarely given a chance. That was his only appearance of the season, he played only once in 1958-59 and was given 5 games in 1959-60. In November 1959, Byrne, now 22 but still playing regular Central League football, was placed on the transfer list along with Louis Bimpson and Alan Arnell. The arrival of Bill Shankly changed that. In 6 seasons Byrne missed only 24 games out of a possible 252. Shankly transformed an apparently unremarkable full-back into one of the finest defenders in his new-look team.

Byrne was ever-present when Liverpool walked away with the Second Division title in 1961-62, missed only 9 games when the Reds won the First Division in 1963-64, and was again ever-present when they lifted the championship again in 1965-66. He was capped by England, against Scotland at Wembley in April 1963, with another cap coming against Norway in Oslo in June 1966. That year he was a member of

Alf Ramsey's victorious World Cup squad but did not play again. As Everton's Ray Wilson filled the number-3 shirt, Byrne watched from the Wembley touchline as England beat West Germany in the final.

A year earlier, though, he had been a Wembley hero with a performance that almost defied belief. In only the third minute of the 1965 FA Cup final, Byrne broke his collarbone in a collision with Leeds United's captain, Bobby Collins. As he put it later, 'Shankly didn't like injuries', and, anyway, Byrne was desperate not to let down his teammates and leave them to play almost the entire match with 10 men. There were no substitutes and so he begged the Reds' trainer, Bob Paisley, not to reveal the extent of his injury. Paisley obliged and Byrne played for 117 minutes – the game cruelly went into extra-time – in agony with 1 arm hanging limply by his side. His heroics did not end there, however. He laid on the cross for Roger Hunt's 93rd-minute goal. Leeds soon equalised but with 3 minutes of extra-time remaining, Ian St John scored the winner.

Had it not been for Byrne, it is doubtful that Liverpool would have won the FA Cup for the first time that year. It was typical of his style. Once he had taken over from Ronnie Moran, whose career was being brought to a close by injuries, he proved to be the most uncompromising of defenders. 'Hard but fair' is perhaps a cliché but in Byrne's case it sums him up perfectly. He had made 330 League and Cup appearances – just a single appearance as a substitute – and scored 1 goal (in the 6-1 European Cup romp against KR Reykjavik in September 1964) before a recurring knee injury ended his playing career. He joined the Liverpool backroom staff and was held in such esteem that in April 1970, a crowd of 41,000 attended his testimonial match at Anfield.

Gerry Byrne died at a Wrexham nursing home on 28 November 2015, suffering from Alzheimer's disease. He was 77.

Bill Shankly

Considering all that has happened since, it is difficult to imagine the state of Liverpool Football Club in 1959. The club could not get out of the Second Division, the Anfield stadium was a rickety old place, training facilities were modest to say the least, and, most important of all, the playing staff was an unwieldy mix of players past their best-before date, youngsters yet to make an impression, and some moderate performers who the Reds really needed to move on. Phil Taylor had tried his best but as Liverpool continued to fall just short of a return to the top flight, the pressure on him proved too much.

But where to look for a new manager? On 19 November, Liverpool chairman Tom Williams and director Sidney Reakes travelled on the midnight train from Liverpool to Glasgow to sign St Mirren's 22-year-old wing-half, Tommy Leishman. Williams was a major figure in what was – if only supporters had known it at the time – the rebirth of their club. In fact, he was something of a football visionary. It was he who brought together Bob Paisley, Reuben Bennett and Joe Fagan who would be the key figures in the famous Anfield bootroom, and it was he who saw the potential in buying the rough school field in West Derby that would be developed into the famous Melwood training base. However, on this occasion he was about to make his greatest contribution to Liverpool FC – and it was not the signing of Leishman, good servant though he would prove.

Applications for the manager's job had been arriving at the club's registered office in Victoria Street. Another director, Lawson Martindale, explained:

> We desire secrecy. That is why we have asked candidates to send their applications to our registered office. Even a postage stamp could indicate the identity of the sender.

We are hopeful that we shall have many first-class men seeking the job, but we do not wish to cause any of them, or their clubs, embarrassment.

Of course, that did not stop the guessing game, and 1 name that kept reoccurring was that of Huddersfield Town's manager, 46-year-old Bill Shankly. Writing in the *Liverpool Echo*, Leslie Edwards said, 'The story goes that if Mr Shankly applies for the position, he stands a very good chance of getting it.'

In fact, Shankly had applied for the job before, back in 1951 when the board decided that he lacked experience and went, instead, for the proven Don Welsh. Eight years later, however, Shankly had established his credentials. A ball-winning wing-half with Carlisle United and Preston North End (with whom he played in 2 FA Cup finals, with a winners' medal in 1938, and was capped for Scotland), Shankly started out in management with Carlisle in March 1949. He hated giving up playing – it never replaced the thrills he felt on the field – and took the Brunton Park club to third place in the Third Division North. The fans there loved him because he took to speaking to them over the public-address system before every match. Turned down by Liverpool, he went to manage Grimsby Town and rejuvenated that club before surprisingly moving to Workington where, again, he turned a bunch of no-hopers into promotion candidates. Then he managed Huddersfield, where he gave the teenage Denis Law a first chance of League football, but, unable to get Huddersfield back into the top flight, he handed in his resignation at Leeds Road, worked a month's notice and joined Liverpool in December 1959 on a salary reported to be £2,500 a year. He told Steve Richards of the *Daily Herald*, 'I'm going to take off my jacket at Liverpool. I'm going to work harder than I've ever worked.'

Richards said that Tom Williams had made £50,000 available to the new manager to buy players for a promotion bid, and the man who had been born and brought up in the harsh surroundings of an Ayrshire mining village was on his way to turning Liverpool into one of the greatest football clubs the game has ever seen. A large number of players were moved out of Anfield but Shankly kept the backroom staff. New players were brought in. Ian St John and Ron Yeats were among the first and they helped Liverpool storm their way to the Second Division title in 1961-62, a success that was followed by 3 League championships, 2 FA Cups, the UEFA Cup and, for good measure, 2 FA Charity Shield wins before, in July 1974, Shankly shocked everyone by announcing his retirement. By then he had laid the foundations for all that would follow under Paisley and then Fagan – another 7 League championships and 4 European Cups in the 10 seasons after Shankly called it a day.

Those foundations included not simply the signings of some great players – when his 1960s' team started to decline, Shankly brought in men such as Kevin Keegan, Steve Heighway, Larry Lloyd and Ray Clemence – but also a complete philosophy. Melwood was transformed into one of the most up-to-date training complexes that football had ever seen. Players' fitness was paramount. When the League was won again in 1965-66, only 14 players were used, and 2 of them played only 5 games between them. The players changed at Anfield, travelled to Melwood for 5-a-side games, and then bussed it back to shower and lunch together. In his 1976 autobiography, *Shankly*, he wrote, 'The socialism I believe in is not really politics. It is a way of living. I believe the only way to live and be truly successful is by collective effort, with everyone working for each other … . It's the way I see football and the way I see life.'

Liverpool – indeed, football – without Shankly was unthinkable. The club's board tried to persuade him to stay, offering him a better contract, but money was not what motivated him. He had made up his mind that he wanted a break from the game that he had graced for so long. But he saw the need for continuity and it was his idea that Bob Paisley, together with Joe Fagan, Reuben Bennett, Ronnie Moran, Roy Evans and Tom Saunders should all move up.

Derby County tempted him back as an advisor for a short while and their then club secretary, Stuart Webb, recalls:

> Dressed in his grey suit and red tie, Bill paced the Derby County dressing room, his face wreathed in a smile, hands thrust deep into his trouser pockets. Every so often, he stooped to growl, 'I want you cutting the front lawn tomorrow, son,' leaving a bemused team asking each other, 'Cutting the front lawn? What on earth is he on about?' You see, Bill was from an era when players came from the

local town, drank in the local pub, their wives shopped locally, and after a good win, those players could get the lawnmower out of the shed on a Sunday afternoon, stick out their chests and give the front lawn a trim, safe in the knowledge of favourable comments from every fan who passed by.

Bill Shankly, who was awarded the OBE, died on 29 September 1981, following a heart attack. He was 68.

Ron Yeats

On 21 October 1961, Liverpool travelled to Derby County. The Reds had started the season in brilliant fashion, winning their first 6 matches and dropping only 3 points from their first 13 games. The previous week, they had crushed Walsall 6-1 at Anfield. So far, they had conceded only 7 goals. Derby, too, had started well, winning 6 and drawing 3 of their first 13 games. They beat Liverpool 2-0 that day, although by the end of the season it was the Reds who had marched away with the Second Division title, with the Derby finishing a distant 16th.

The Baseball Ground match had been marked by a stunning long-range goal from Derby's 19-year-old wing-half Mick Hopkinson, but it is better remembered locally for a couple of incidents involving Liverpool's giant centre-half Ron Yeats. Liverpool were taking a corner when Bill Curry, scorer of Derby's second goal, ended up writhing on the halfway line. Yeats had been the nearest Liverpool player. Minutes later, the Liverpool centre-half bundled Derby's number 9 into the Popular Side railings and he was stretchered off. The *Daily Herald* reported, 'Home supporters invaded the pitch, brandishing their fists at Yeats.' At the end, hundreds of fans – home and away supporters – surged over the ground and a youth aimed a kick at Yeats. The fisticuffs spilled over into the nearby Midland Railway Station. Remarkably, no arrests were made but the afternoon's events moved the *Daily Mail* to call the affair 'the scourge of soccer'. In the *Liverpool Echo*, Michael Charters defended Yeats:

> I gathered afterwards that Curry, a provocative type of player, had stood in Yeats's path as the Liverpool player started to run upfield. When the 14st of Yeats is on the move, something has to go … . Yeats was booed whenever the ball went near him in the next couple of minutes,

and then came the major incident ... . In my book, Yeats had been scrupulously fair all through a fierce game against some provocation. His tackle on Curry, the spark which started the explosion, was carried through with all the force of his big frame, but it was not a foul.

Ron Yeats was certainly an uncompromising type of centre-half, which is why Bill Shankly bought the 23 year old from Dundee United for £20,000 in July 1961. He was a massive presence in every way, spending a decade at Anfield and captaining the Reds to 3 trophies – the League championship, the FA Cup, and then the League title again – before he left to become player-assistant manager of Tranmere Rovers in December 1971. The Aberdeen-born defender and former apprentice slaughterman stood 6ft 2ins tall, and, as Charters said, when he was on the move, nothing was allowed to impede his progress. Even the first of the 15 goals he would score for Liverpool was momentous: it came in the 75th minute of the First Division match at Old Trafford on 23 November 1963 and was enough to beat Manchester United, who failed to score that afternoon. At the end of the season, Liverpool sat on top of the First Division, 4 points ahead of United.

Yeats played twice for Scotland and there were commentators on the game who thought he should have won many more caps. After making 450 starts for Liverpool – and coming on once as a substitute – he went across the Mersey and soon moved up to become player-manager Tranmere, and then player-manager of Stalybridge Celtic, and Barrow. He played in the American Soccer League (not to be confused with the North American Soccer League) with Los Angeles Skyhawks and Santa Barbara Condors, and ended his playing days with Formby and Rhyl before being appointed Liverpool's chief scout, a role in which he remained until retiring in May 2006. In April 2009, the Lord Mayor of Liverpool bestowed on Yeats – who was Liverpool's longest-serving captain until Steven Gerrard surpassed that record – the award of Honorary Scouser. The man whom Bill Shankly dubbed 'The Colossus' is, like so many players of his generation, now suffering from Alzheimer's disease.

Ian Callaghan

Eighteen-year-old Ian Callaghan blushed as teammates and spectators alike applauded him off the pitch at the end of Liverpool's 4-0 win over Bristol Rovers at Anfield on 16 April 1960. Callaghan, who stood 5ft 7ins, was the ninth player tried in the outside-right position by Liverpool that season, and at last it seemed that the Reds had found someone who could fill the role. Callaghan's was the happiest of debuts, and, according to Leslie Edwards of the *Liverpool Echo*, not since Billy Liddell had Liverpool found a youngster of comparable promise: 'Callaghan is a mere boy in looks but possesses a surprisingly mature body and with legs to match and a brain which enables him to do many common-sense things.' Edwards said that he would not rate Callaghan as a 'second Matthews, but he does show much promise and while he elects not to accept the direct duel with the back, he will continue to have time to learn and develop'.

Good judge of a footballer as he obviously was, it is doubtful that even Leslie Edwards, nor anyone else for that matter, could have imagined that Ian Callaghan, whose first senior appearance had come after only 4 games for the reserves in the Central League, would still be playing for Liverpool 18 years later, by which time he would have clocked up a club record 848 appearances in League, FA Cup, League Cup and European football. Only 5 of them would be as a substitute; indeed, the use of substitutes was still in the future when the teenage Callaghan made his bow. He scored 69 goals for Liverpool. By the time he played his final game, on 29 March 1978, in the second leg of the European Cup semi-final against Borussia Mönchengladbach at Anfield, he was the only Liverpool player whose career had gone from the Reds' attempts to get out of the Second Division at the start of the 1960s to European champions.

The Toxteth-born player, who first joined Liverpool as an amateur in 1957, could look back on a treasure trove of honours: 5 League championship medals (and 4 runners-up medals); 2 FA Cup winners' medals; 1 Second Division championship medal; 2 European Cup winners' medals; 2 UEFA Cup winners' medals; 1 UEFA Super Cup winners' medal; 4 FA Charity Shield winners' medals; 4 England caps; 2 appearances for the Football League; 1 Footballer of the Year award. It was an astonishing haul. He also played in a European Cup-winners' Cup final and a Football League Cup final, both of which Liverpool lost. One of his England caps came in the 1966 World Cup finals, against France at Wembley, and he holds the record for the longest period between caps, with 11 years and 49 days between his second and third appearances. He was also awarded the MBE.

Despite that hugely impressive debut, Bill Shankly had carefully nursed him and it would be the promotion of 1961-62 before he became a regular with 24 games that season. Thereafter, only injury kept him out of the team (he missed much of 1970-71 because of a cartilage operation) as he found his role in midfield. Callaghan was 36 when he finally lost his place in the Liverpool first team. In recognition of his long and distinguished service, the club gave him a free transfer, and, after spending the summer in the North American Soccer League (NASL) with Fort Lauderdale Strikers, he joined his former Liverpool teammate, John Toshack, at Third Division Swansea City in September 1978. He made 76 League appearances for Swansea, helping them to win promotion as well as the Welsh Cup. There were short spells in Australian soccer with Canberra City, at Cork City in the League of Ireland – and he would have played for the Norwegian club Sandefjord BK but could not obtain a work permit – before he ended his playing career with 15 appearances for Crewe Alexandra, by which time he was in his 40th year and an Achilles tendon injury finally brought down the curtain on a remarkable football career.

Gordon Milne

Bill Shankly knew all about Gordon Milne. Milne's father, Jimmy, and Shankly were neighbours during their playing days. So, on 30 August 1960, the Liverpool manager knew exactly the sort of player – and person – he was getting when he signed the son of Preston North End's trainer for £16,000 from the Deepdale club.

Twenty-three-year-old Milne's Liverpool debut came in the home Second Division match against Southampton. It was a less than happy first appearance because the Saints won 1-0, but it was the start of a fine Liverpool career.

Preston born and bred, Milne, it was felt by locals, would do better away from his hometown club. The *Liverpool Echo's* Leslie Edwards said that someone who knew Milne well had told him, 'He is a charming man, a good team man, a right-thinking boy. He neither smokes nor drinks.' Everton's Alex Parker, who had played with Milne in the British Army team, said, 'I know that he is only small, but he is one of the best men I know at building up an attack. After a few matches I know that you Koppites will agree with me.' Indeed, they did.

Milne had started his career with Preston Amateurs and Morecambe before signing for Preston in 1956. He played in a handful of matches before replacing Tommy Docherty in the side in 1958-59 but was perhaps made a scapegoat for Preston's poor start to 1960-61 – they were relegated that season – and a few days after being dropped he was his way to Anfield and a fresh start.

He made 16 appearances in his first season with Liverpool but when the Reds were promoted in 1961-62 he never missed a game. He was marked absent only once in 1962-63 – because he was making his full England debut, against Brazil at Wembley. Liverpool were playing Birmingham City that evening – the Reds won 5-1 – and England youth international Tommy Smith made his first appearance in the team in place of Milne. There were no 'international breaks' in those days.

When the League championship was won in 1963-64, Milne was again an ever-present, and another First Division medal followed in 1965-66, when he played only 28 times in a season ruined for Milne by an injury that ultimately cost him a place in Alf Ramsey's World Cup squad. Injury had also kept Milne out of the 1965 FA Cup final; a similar fate had befallen his father when Preston reached Wembley in 1938 and he broke his collarbone a week before the final. In Milne's case, it was a tackle by Chelsea's Eddie McCreadie that cost him a medal. When Liverpool lost 4-0 at Stamford Bridge on Good Friday, 17 April, the Liverpool player had to leave the field after only 22 minutes. He returned with his right leg heavily strapped and limped off for good with 18 minutes remaining. Liverpool worked hard to get him fit for Wembley but the damage to his ligaments proved too serious.

Despite being a regular member of the Liverpool team in 1966-67, at the end of that season, Milne was sold to Second Division Blackpool for £32,000. The Seasiders' manager, Stan Mortensen, was keen to sign him after Blackpool's shock 3-1 at Anfield on the last day of the season. Milne had made 279 appearances (including 2 as a substitute) for Liverpool and scored 19 goals for the Reds. Shankly said, 'There is no doubt that Gordon Milne was one of my best-ever signings. Gordon is a great clubman who has given us excellent service and never a moment's anxiety or trouble. I am certain that he will do splendidly with Blackpool.'

Milne, who won 14 caps while with Liverpool, spent 2 seasons at Bloomfield Road before becoming player-manager of Northern Premier League club Wigan Athletic. He managed the England youth team and he was a successful manager of both Coventry City and Leicester City, worked in Turkey (where he was again hugely successful) and Japan, was chief executive of the League Managers' Association, and Bobby Robson's director of football at Newcastle United.

Ian St John

On 15 August 1959, Motherwell's Ian St John scored what is still the fastest hat-trick in Scottish football's history. He had the ball in the net 3 times in 2 minutes and 30 seconds in a League Cup match against Hibernian. On 9 May 1961, St John scored a hat-trick for Liverpool at Goodison Park. The first goal was just before half-time, when a back pass from Brian Harris eluded Everton goalkeeper Albert Dunlop and rebounded off a post for St John to slam home. Five minutes after the interval, Ian Callaghan crossed for St John to take the ball on the half turn and steer into the net. One minute from the end, St John chased a through ball from Roger Hunt, brushed aside Brian Labone and hammered home from 12 yards.

It was 'only' the Liverpool Senior Cup final, but pride was still at stake (as it turned out Everton won, 4-3). It was also Ian St John's debut. Michael Charters said in the *Liverpool Echo*, 'St John is the type of player Liverpool fans have wanted to see at Anfield for years.'

Born in Motherwell on 7 June 1938, in April 1952, he watched Motherwell beat Dundee 4-0 to win the Scottish Cup for the first time. Five years later, after playing for Motherwell Bridge Works and Douglas Water Thistle, he signed for the Steelmen, and over the next 4 years terrorised defences, scoring 80 goals in only 113 League matches before Bill Shankly signed him for what was then the biggest transfer fee that Liverpool had ever paid out – £37,500. He was already an international, winning the first of 21 caps – he scored 9 goals for Scotland – when he was only 20.

Standing only 5ft 7ins tall, St John was on the small side for a striker, but that hardly mattered. His debut against Everton had shown that he could score goals and that he could withstand a battering from bigger and heavier defenders. In his first 3 seasons at Anfield he missed only 6 League games out of a possible 120. Only in 1964-65 did he miss many games through injury. Then he picked up again and in the next 4 seasons was absent only 6 times out of 168 games. When Liverpool were promoted in 1961-62, he scored 18 League goals to finish second in the list behind Roger Hunt – no one was going to get anywhere near Hunt's tally of 41 goals in as many matches – and when the First Division championship was won in 1963-64, he scored 21 goals, this time only 10 behind the remarkable Hunt. The championship-winning season of 1965-66 saw St John score 10 times. Hunt got 30. They were a formidable strike partnership. With his exquisite ball control and timing St John was both a maker and a taker of goals. In the thick of it up front, or behind the goalmouth frenzy, setting things up from deeper.

In May 1965, however, St John had the stage to himself. It was Hunt who opened the scoring in extra-time of the FA Cup final against Leeds United, but after Billy Bremner's equaliser, it was St John who acrobatically headed home Callaghan's cross to bring the FA Cup to Anfield for the very first time.

In the 1971 close season he played in South Africa, for Hellenic FC, before signing for Coventry City that August. His 424 games for Liverpool (419 starts) had yielded 118 goals. However he was, he wrote in his autobiography, disappointed by the way that it ended: 'Bill Shankly had dropped me without saying a word, without even meeting my eyes.' He ended his playing career with Tranmere Rovers who were then managed by Ron Yeats. St John managed Motherwell and Portsmouth, assisted Coventry City and Sheffield Wednesday, and then carved out a successful media career, in part with his contemporary, Jimmy Greaves. In 2014, he announced that he had undergone surgery for cancer, and in 2017 revealed that, like so many footballers of his generation, he was suffering from problems with his memory.

Tommy Lawrence

When Phil Taylor signed 17-year-old goalkeeper Tommy Lawrence as a professional on 30 September 1957, Tommy Younger was the king between the posts. Then Bert Slater took over with Younger going to Falkirk, as player-manager, in exchange. Occasionally, Doug Rudham got back in the team. Then Jim Furnell, who came from Burnley. Finally, on 27 October 1962, Lawrence got his chance.

Liverpool lost 1-0 to West Brom at The Hawthorns that day, but it was no fault of their goalkeeper. In the *Liverpool Echo*, Horace Yates wrote:

> Tommy Lawrence will not let Liverpool down, if his debut provided a sample of his worth. When recently we have seen so many goalkeepers ... handle the ball as though it were red hot, how comforting it was to see Lawrence take it with all the assurance of an expert slip fielder at cricket.

Tommy Lawrence's long wait was over. After that impressive start, he was Liverpool's automatic choice until Ray Clemence took over 8 years later. In 6 seasons Lawrence missed only 4 matches, won League championship medals in 1963-64 and 1965-66, and an FA Cup winners' medal in 1964-65. In 1963, he won the first of 3 Scotland caps – the other 2 came after Clemence had replaced him – and in 1968-69 he conceded only 24 goals in 42 First Division matches. That says as much about Liverpool's dominance, but it was still a record for a goalkeeper, one that Clemence equalled and was later broken. Lawrence was dubbed the 'Flying Pig' by Liverpool's fans, an affectionate nod to the way he threw himself around the penalty area despite weighing over 14 stone.

Born in the Ayrshire village of Dailly on 14 May 1940, Lawrence was playing for Warrington Town when Phil Taylor first signed him, in September 1956. Twelve months later, he brought the professional goalkeeping strength on Liverpool's books to 3. The Reds had been living dangerously when it came to cover in that position.

On 21 February 1970, Liverpool lost a sixth-round FA Cup-tie 1-0 to Second Division Watford at Vicarage Road. Clemence came in for the next game. Lawrence next appeared on 26 April 1971, in a 2-2 draw at Maine Road where both clubs fielded weakened teams because they faced European games 2 days hence. It was the last of the 387 League, Cup and European appearances that Lawrence made for Liverpool.

On 30 September 1971, now 31, he joined Third Division Tranmere Rovers. It was a slightly complicated transfer. Lawrence went to Prenton Park in exchange for their goalkeeper, 23-year-old Wallasey-born Frankie Lane, with Rovers also receiving £15,000. Tranmere valued Lane at £30,000 but they had to sell to remain in business. Ostensibly, Lawrence went on a 3-month loan with the FA's blessing that if he was needed by Liverpool for a European tie, then he could return to Anfield. At the end of the 3 months, once Lane had become eligible to play in Europe for the Reds, then the Lawrence transfer would be made permanent. Tranmere's general manager, Dave Russell, said, 'We've sold a very good goalkeeper in Lane, and obtained another one in Lawrence – who can give us years of fine service – and collected cash as well – cash that is absolutely vital to us at present.' Neither player knew of the move until they reported for training that morning.

Lawrence added another 80 League appearances for Tranmere, where Ron Yeats became his manager, before being released at the end of the 1973-74 season. In August 1974, he signed for Cheshire League club, Chorley, where he ended his playing days.

In February 2015, a BBC reporter, conducting vox pops, asked a man if he remembered the 1967 Merseyside derby at Goodison Park. 'I played in it,' was the reply. 'I was goalkeeper for Liverpool. It was a great game.'

Tommy Lawrence died on 10 January 2018. He was 77. When his coffin, draped in a red LFC banner, left St Elphin's Church in Warrington, *You'll Never Walk Alone* was played and mourners applauded a great Liverpool player.

Peter Thompson

In 1958, Peter Thompson was a schoolboy star with caps for England against West Germany, Scotland and Wales. When the time came for him to leave school, League club scouts flocked to the door of the Carlisle boy. First Division Preston North End won the race, and Thompson was still only 17 when made his First Division debut, on 30 August 1960, against Arsenal. By the end of the season he was Preston's leading scorer, albeit with only 12 League and Cup goals in a relegation season. He was ever-present for the next 2 seasons, and made a special impression on Bill Shankly in February 1962, when he scored the winner in an FA Cup fifth-round second replay against Liverpool at Old Trafford. Preston, still drifting in the Second Division, could not hold on to such a talent and in the 1963 close season, Liverpool beat off Everton, Wolves and even Juventus, to sign Thompson for £40,000.

Shankly, it appeared, had been eyeing up the player for some years. A Carlisle schoolmaster, Mick Hamilton, had tipped him off about a brilliant 15-year-old footballer, but Huddersfield Town, whom Shankly was then managing, could not lure him to Leeds Road. Preston, of course, wanted to keep him at Deepdale, but Thompson had become unsettled, not just because Preston were playing in the second tier, but also because they had played him in several forward positions other than his favourite outside-left spot. He asked for a transfer and when it became obvious that he was never going to change his mind, Preston faced up to the inevitable and settled for the big fee instead.

There was now a spring in the step of everyone at Anfield. The Reds had an exciting new player, the new cantilevered Kemlyn Road stand was a great addition to the old ground, and the press were happy with their new accommodation, even though it was now only half as big. Everyone's optimism was well-founded, especially when it came to Peter Thompson. In his first season, 1963-64, the right-footed left-winger played in every game as Liverpool topped the First Division. Two years later, Liverpool won the title again with Thompson missing only 2 League matches. In between he won an FA Cup winners' medal.

There were plenty of highlights, none more memorable than the day in April 1964 when Liverpool confirmed themselves as champions with a 5-0 drubbing of Arsenal at Anfield. Thompson scored 2 of the goals: cutting inside and hammering home from 12 yards out; then popping up in the inside-right spot to lob the ball over the head of goalkeeper Jim Furnell, who had been transferred from Anfield to Highbury 5 months earlier. In the *Daily Mirror*, Frank McGhee said, 'The Kop set the match to music and sang their team to the championship with a wit and a warmth woven so closely it became a part of the game itself. Liverpool fans don't just watch a game. They take part. They live it.'

Such rare talent as Thompson's was always going to be rewarded by full international recognition and he won 16 caps. He was twice selected for an initial World Cup squad, in 1966 and 1970, but didn't make the final cut on either occasion. Ramsey did without wingers. For Liverpool, Thompson began the 1970-71 season in the first team, but then suffered a cartilage injury at Huddersfield just before Christmas and missed most of the remainder of the season, although he did come off the bench to replace Alun Evans in the 1971 FA Cup final defeat by Arsenal.

In January 1974, after 6 weeks on loan at Burnden Park, Thompson was transferred to Bolton Wanderers for £18,000. He had made 404 starts and 8 substitute appearances for Liverpool and scored 54 goals for the Reds. He played 132 times for Bolton, helping them to promotion to the First Division in 1977-78 before retiring at the end of that season. After football, he ran a caravan park and hotels.

Peter Thompson died on 31 December 2018. He was 76.

Chris Lawler

On 24 November 1973, Chris Lawler suffered a knee injury while playing for Liverpool at QPR. After 29 minutes he had to leave the field, to be replaced by Phil Boersma. It looked bad and, 2 days later, Bill Shankly confirmed what everyone had feared at the time: Lawler, Liverpool's right-back for 395 League games, would miss his first through injury since a match against Tottenham Hotspur at White Hart Lane in September 1965. Since then, he had missed only 1 match, through design rather than injury when he was 1 of several first-teamers rested against Manchester City in April 1971, 2 days before Liverpool met Leeds United in the second leg of their Fairs Cup semi-final. After the Loftus Road game, Shankly said, 'He's been told to stay at home until the pain has eased. Then we'll decide what to do.' In fact, Lawler played only one more League game that season. The curtain was beginning to come down on a wonderful Liverpool career.

Lawler was born in Liverpool on 20 October 1943. He signed for the Reds as an amateur in May 1959 and became a professional in October 1960, the month he added England youth caps to those he had won as a schoolboy. Having captained his country at under-15 level, he now led England's under 18s.

A year later he was a regular at centre-half in Liverpool's reserve team in the Central League, and in March 1963 he made his first-team debut, in a 2-2 draw with West Bromwich Albion at Anfield. He played in 5 more League games that season, and in another 6 in 1963-64, when Liverpool won the First Division. Shortly into the 1964-65 season he came back into the team, and there he remained, Liverpool's first-choice right-back for the next 10 seasons until that injury at Loftus Road.

The honours just flowed: 3 Football League championship medals; 2 FA Cup winners' medals; 1 UEFA Cup winners' medal; and runners-up in the European Cup-winners' Cup, the FA Cup and in the First Division, and 4 FA Charity Shield matches.

Altogether, Lawler would play in 546 League, Cup and European matches for Liverpool. Just as impressive – perhaps more so as he was a defender – was his tally of goals – 61. He even scored on his full England debut, 1 of 4 caps he won at that level. His ability to arrive, unannounced, in the opposition penalty area, earned him the nickname 'Silent Knight'.

His great friend was Tommy Smith and it was ironic that Lawler's injury, in April 1973, let Smith back into the team, 3 weeks after he had been dropped. The knee injury resulted in Lawler, who was now 30 years old, undergoing a cartilage operation, and he was never the same player after that. Shankly rewarded him by selecting him as a substitute for the 1974 FA Cup final against Newcastle United, which meant that he qualified for a winners' medal even though he did not play in the match.

In October 1975, he moved to Portsmouth, who were then managed by Ian St John. It was a reluctant decision on Lawler's behalf. Liverpool had given him a free transfer but he initially told his former teammate that he had no desire to drop down into the Second Division with a move to Fratton Park. He explained to the *Liverpool Echo*, 'Portsmouth is a long way away and although Ian is disappointed, he understood the situation. I've told Bob Paisley the decision as well, and he says that if any clubs are interested in me, even if they are in the First Division, he is willing to let me go.' A couple of weeks later, however, Lawler had a change of heart.

Alas, he could not help keep Portsmouth up, and they dropped into the Third Division. He made 36 League appearances for them before ending his playing career with Stockport County and Bangor City, and in the USA. After coaching in Norway and working for Wigan Athletic, he coached Liverpool's reserve team for several years.

Tommy Smith

No Liverpool player has surely ever felt closer to the club than Tommy Smith, who was born only a few hundred yards from Anfield, on 5 April 1945. The family's only child, when he was 14 his father died from pneumonia. It was at Anfield that he found a purpose, which was not surprising since his father and his grandfather were both staunch Liverpool supporters.

Smith joined the Reds as an amateur in 1960. His mother told Bill Shankly to 'to take good care of him'. He turned professional on his 17th birthday and he was always going to be a special player. Shankly could see that. When other 15 year olds were playing at the fourth and fifth levels, Smith went straight into the club's third team. It would be a few years before Shankly would pronounce: 'Tommy Smith wasn't born – he was quarried,' but the strength and the commitment were there from the beginning.

He made his League debut in the final home game of the 1962-63 season, a 5-1 win over Birmingham City. He might not have been available had the Reds had to play their FA Youth Cup quarter-final on the same day, but the game had been switched to the following day at the Blades' request.

In the *Liverpool Echo*, Michael Charters said:

> Liverpool did so well with 3 reserves – with them, not despite them, for the performance of the youngsters Tommy Smith, Lawler and Wallace showed how well placed the club is for the future. Smith, on his League debut, played with astonishing maturity and will be a powerhouse of a player one day.

A few days later, Ron Yeats, writing in the same newspaper, said, 'Tommy Smith, for instance, is a big, strong, hard-grafting lad.'

Incidentally, Liverpool won that FA Youth Cup match against Sheffield United and went on to meet West Ham United in the final where they lost 6-5 on aggregate to a Hammers team that included Harry Redknapp. That same season, Smith captained the England team that won the European under-18 championship.

He did not feature in Liverpool's first team in 1963-64, as the League championship was won, but the following season he made 25 League appearances and won an FA Cup winners' medal. It was the first of many club honours, although his solitary England cap should have been more. During his Liverpool career, he won 4 League championship medals, 2 FA Cup winners' medals, 1 European Cup winners' medal, 2 UEFA Cup medals, and 1 UEFA Super Cup medal. That list covers so many highlights but perhaps the most memorable was his decisive goal in the 1977 European Cup final against Borussia Mönchengladbach. It gave Liverpool a 2-1 lead and they won 3-1.

Starting out as a full-back, he moved into the centre of defence. Brian Glanville said in *The Guardian* that Tommy Smith was 'more in the manner of Bobby Moore than of Jack Charlton', a player who 'married skill with terror'. Not for nothing was Smith known as 'The Anfield Iron', but, as Glanville said, 'He was not just a forceful tackler and an implacable marker; he was also a shrewd reader of the game and an accurate user of the ball.'

After the European Cup triumph, he had 1 more season at Anfield before signing for Swansea City, where John Toshack was manager. He had made 632 starts for Liverpool – and come on once as a substitute – and scored 48 goals for the Reds. Alas, there had been rumblings for some time, and in 1973 Smith lost the Liverpool captaincy after complaining to Shankly when he was dropped for a match against Arsenal.

Smith, who was awarded the MBE for services to football, also played in the NASL before retiring in 1979. He had a spell as a coach at Liverpool and also wrote a popular column for the *Liverpool Echo*. He suffered a number of ailments and in October 2014 he was diagnosed with Alzheimer's disease. He died in a Crosby nursing home on 12 April 2019, aged 74.

Ray Clemence

The signing was given the briefest mention in the *Liverpool Echo*. A single paragraph in June 1967, announcing that an 18-year-old goalkeeper had been transferred from Scunthorpe United to Liverpool for a 5-figure fee and that, despite his age, the previous season he had made 46 appearances for the Iron including 2 FA Cup ties. Skegness-born Ray Clemence arrived at Anfield largely unheralded. Who was going to oust Tommy Lawrence? He had missed only 4 League matches in the past 4 seasons, and, indeed, would be ever-present in the First Division for the next 2.

The signing of a teenage goalkeeper unknown outside the Third Division was not headline news, even if Liverpool had paid £18,000 for him. After regular first-team football at the Old Showground, Clemence was to serve a lengthy apprenticeship at Anfield. The day of his debut eventually arrived in the shape of a Football League Cup-tie at home to Swansea Town in September 1968. A year later, he played in Europe but even that was no opportunity to show what he could do. He played in both legs of a first-round tie against League of Ireland club, Dundalk, but Liverpool won 14-0 on aggregate, and when the Reds faced Vitória de Setúbal in the next round, Lawrence returned for the serious stuff.

Finally, Clemence was given his League debut in January 1970, at Nottingham Forest. Again, Lawrence was back for the next match, but that turned out to be an FA Cup quarter-final defeat at the hands of Second Division Watford. Bill Shankly was already beginning to dismantle the team that had brought Liverpool such success in the 1960s. Seven days after the humiliating Cup defeat, Shankly made changes for the visit of Brian Clough's Derby County. Out went Tommy Lawrence, Ian St John, Ron Yeats and Ian Ross. Back from injury came Peter Thompson and Tommy Smith. In came Clemence and midfielder Doug Livermore. Liverpool won 2-0 – Dave Mackay scored an own-goal – and Clemence was established as the Reds' number-1 goalkeeper. He remained in the team for the rest of that season, and in the next 11 years missed only 6 League games. In 1970-71, Liverpool equalled the record they had set in 1968-69 when they conceded only 24 goals in a 42-match League season. Clemence missed only 1 game and let in 22 goals; Lawrence let in the other 2. In 1978-78, Clemence was ever-present as Liverpool conceded only 16 goals, only 1 more than Preston had conceded in the League's first season of 1888-89, in only 20 matches.

Naturally, Clemence's honours list is impressive: 5 League championships; 1 FA Cup (and another final); 1 Football League Cup; 3 European Cups (and 5 finals in all); 2 UEFA Cups; 1 UEFA Super Cup; 5 FA Charity Shields. He was the most dependable of goalkeepers in a team of hugely dependable and consistent players, and his positional sense was remarkable. His England career spanned 12 years and 61 caps, which would have been more but for the presence of Peter Shilton. He also became the first goalkeeper to captain England since Frank Swift.

In August 1981, after making 656 senior appearances for Liverpool, despite the fact that he still had 2 years left on his contract at Anfield, Clemence, now 33, asked for a transfer. Bob Paisley was reluctant to let him go but Clemence had made up his mind. He moved to Spurs for £300,000.

His last game for Liverpool was the 1981 European Cup final victory over Real Madrid in Paris. His first appearance for Spurs was at Wembley in the FA Charity Shield draw with Aston Villa, and, at White Hart Lane, Clemence added FA Cup and UEFA Cup medals to his haul of honours. He retired in April 1988 and has since coached at Spurs, managed Barnet, and held senior positions in the England set-up before retiring as the FA's head of national teams in 2013. Clemence, who, in 1987, was awarded the MBE for service to football, has for some years been suffering from prostate cancer.

Emlyn Hughes

In late February 1967, the sports pages were full of the comings and goings – actually it was just comings – at Anfield. Bill Shankly had signed Preston North End winger Davie Wilson for £20,000, and was now rumoured to be looking to sign wing-half Howard Kendall from Preston for £80,000. Wilson and Kendall had played in the 1964 FA Cup final for Preston. Wilson, though, found Ian Callaghan's grip on the outside-right shirt immovable. Fifteen months later he was back at Deepdale with Liverpool losing £16,000 on the deal. Kendall, of course, ended up elsewhere.

There was another incoming transfer that happened that month, one that proved to be one of the most successful of a long list of successes that Shankly engineered for Liverpool. On 27 February 1967, they shattered the British record for a full-back when they paid Blackpool £65,000 for 19-year-old Emlyn Hughes. It was getting on for twice what Arsenal had paid West Brom for Don Howe 3 years earlier. It was also a club record for Liverpool, £25,000 more than they paid Preston for Peter Thompson in August 1963.

Hughes, who was born in Barrow-in-Furness on 28 August 1947 – his father, Fred, was a Great Britain Rugby League international – had made only 28 League appearances for Blackpool, but that was enough for Shankly to want the player in his team. In fact, 12 months earlier, he had offered £25,000 but was turned down by Blackpool's manager Ron Suart. Suart resigned in January 1967 – the Seasiders were heading for relegation from the First Division – and while there was a change of managers (the incoming Stan Mortensen was facing the mammoth task of keeping Blackpool up) he pounced and got his man, the fee now too big to be refused by a club that needed to buy 'men who can beat the opposing defenders and have a go,' according to Mortensen.

Hughes made his Liverpool debut on 4 March 1967, at home to Stoke City. Although primarily a full-back, he was a versatile footballer who could also play at centre-back and in midfield, and against the Potters he was asked to provide the main link in midfield. In the *Liverpool Echo*, Jack Rowe said:

> Not all his tackles were as good as his first. Some had a touch of crudity about them, but straightaway Hughes fell into the Liverpool mould of always busy and always working. He passed calmly and accurately, and I think he came out of his first test with as high marks as any other Liverpool player.

Rowe said that time would tell whether Shankly's assessment that Hughes would play for England would materialise. In fact, Hughes would play 62 times for his country, 23 of them as captain. Naturally, he also skippered Liverpool – notably, leading them to victory in the 1977 European Cup final – and made 657 senior appearances for the Reds, scoring 48 goals, before signing for Wolves in August 1979, for £90,000, when he was 32 and approaching the twilight of his playing career. With Liverpool, he won 4 League championships, 1 FA Cup, 2 European Cups, 2 UEFA Cups, 1 UEFA Super Cup and 3 FA Charity Shields. He also played in losing finals in the FA Cup (twice), Football League Cup and UEFA Super Cup. With Wolves, he won the Football League Cup in 1980.

In July 1981, he became player-manager of Rotherham United, and played for Hull City, Mansfield Town and Swansea City before retiring in October 1983. He was awarded the OBE in 1980, for services to sport, and was voted Footballer of the Year in 1977.

After his playing days were over, Hughes became a familiar face on television, including football punditry but most famously as a team captain in BBC's long-running series *A Question of Sport*. In 2002, he became a presenter and pundit on the nightly football phone-in on Real Radio Yorkshire.

Emlyn Hughes, who did much charitable work, died at his home at Dore, Sheffield, on 9 November 2004. He had been suffering from a brain tumour. He was 57.

Larry Lloyd

In August 1968, 19-year-old, 6ft 3ins tall centre-half Larry Lloyd made his debut for Bristol Rovers. Lloyd played 43 times that season as Rovers finished 16th in the Third Division. He would have been an ever-present but for the fact that, in April 1969, Liverpool paid £50,000 for a young defender who was still in his first season of League football.

Bill Shankly introduced Lloyd slowly. He made his League debut on 27 September 1969, at West Brom where he stood in for Ron Yeats, who was suffering from both a back injury and a cold. He did well enough in a 2-2 draw, and 3 days later, made his debut in European football, albeit in a Fairs Cup first-round tie where Liverpool were already leading Dundalk 10-0 from the first leg. Shankly was impressed, though. He said of Lloyd and goalkeeper Ray Clemence, 'Here are two lads who could be good for at least ten years' service with Liverpool.' The League of Ireland opposition that night provided no sterner challenge than Lloyd and Clemence were accustomed to facing in the Central League, but it was all very encouraging.

Lloyd made only 8 League appearances that season, but in 1970-71 – now partnering Tommy Smith, who was just about the only player to have survived Shankly's rebuilding plans as the team that had prospered through the 1960s was dismantled – he missed only 2 matches in the First Division. The Reds finished fifth in the table and reached the FA Cup final where they went down to Bertie Mee's double-winning Arsenal. The same month, Sir Alf Ramsey gave Lloyd his full England debut, against Wales at Wembley in a side that included his Anfield teammates Chris Lawler, Emlyn Hughes and Tommy Smith, who was also making his international debut.

When Liverpool won the Football League championship and UEFA Cup double in 1972-73, Lloyd did not miss a game, which meant that he played in every minute of the 54 matches. In the first leg of the UEFA Cup final, against Borussia Mönchengladbach at Anfield, he scored Liverpool's third goal, heading home a Kevin Keegan corner in the 63rd minute to give the Reds a solid lead to take to Germany, where they lost 2-0 but lifted the trophy on aggregate.

The following season, however, Lloyd was injured against Norwich City. In the 65th-minute of the match against the Canaries at Anfield on 2 February 1974, he left the field with a thigh muscle injury and did not return. Peter Cormack, the man who replaced him, scored the winner for Liverpool, in the 89th minute, the only goal of the game.

It was the last of Larry Lloyd's 217 senior appearances for Liverpool (he scored 5 goals). The injury dogged him for the remainder of the season. In August 1974, he was not included in the party of 15 players that travelled to Germany for the pre-season friendly against Bundesliga club, 1. FC Kaiserslautern.

On 15 August, Lloyd was transferred to Coventry City for a reported £240,000, a record for both clubs. New Liverpool manager Bob Paisley told the *Liverpool Echo*:

> I leant over backwards to keep Lloyd. He was offered a contract that was out of this world ... . He knew he wouldn't have been in the first team right away. But I asked him to stay in the squad and fight his way back ... . But I couldn't get anywhere with him – he just didn't want to know my point of view. So when Coventry came along with this magnificent offer...

Lloyd made 50 League appearances for cash-strapped Coventry before Brian Clough took him on loan for Nottingham Forest in September 1976, the deal made permanent a month later for £60,000. Lloyd made 148 League appearances for Forest, winning 2 European Cups, 1 League championship, 2 Football League Cups and 1 European Super Cup to add to the League championship and UEFA Cup that he had won with Liverpool. He played in the NASL and ended his career as player-manager of Wigan Athletic, winning them promotion from the Fourth Division.

Steve Heighway

In February 1970, Liverpool and Everton were reported to be battling it out to sign Cheshire League club Skelmersdale United's 22-year-old Dublin-born forward Steve Heighway. Liverpool coach Ronnie Moran had watched him play a starring role in Skelmersdale's FA Amateur Cup quarter-final draw with Slough, and the Reds looked favourites to sign him once the cup run ended.

Heighway's parents were English and had moved back to England when he was 10. He represented Cheshire and England grammar schools, and English universities, and played for an FA XI against the Amateur Football Alliance. Halfway through the 1970-71 season, he and Alan Swift had between them scored 47 of Skem's 79 goals, but it was Heighway, a high-stepping, athletic attacker, who had really caught the eye. Poor Swift would break a leg that April and still not be fit at the start of the following season.

Heighway, meanwhile, was definitely going places. Coventry City served the statutory 7 days' notice that they were going to approach him, and besides the Merseyside clubs, Leeds United were also interested. Skelmersdale, though, were only 2 games away from Wembley. The professional clubs, it seemed, would have to wait, but minutes before he took the field for the replay against Slough, Heighway, the hottest property in amateur football, signed for the Reds, still an unpaid player until Skem's cup adventure ended, which it did with a semi-final defeat by Enfield at Derby.

Heighway had his first taste of League football for Liverpool against West Brom at The Hawthorns on 29 August 1970, when he came on for Peter Thompson after 63 minutes. His first full start came in the League Cup second-round replay against Mansfield Town on 22 September. The very next day he made his full international debut for the Republic of Ireland against Poland at Dalymount Park. It was the first of 34 caps.

Six months earlier, he had been studying for his final exams at Warwick University, from where he graduated with a BA in Politics and Economics. It was a remarkable time for the former amateur star that Liverpool fans would dub 'Big Bamber' after the host of television's *University Challenge*, Bamber Gascoigne (Liverpool teammate and fellow graduate Brian Hall became 'Little Bamber'.)

Heighway's style was that of a strong, fast outside-left, skilful with both feet, a player who, it was said, 'ran with the ball, not after it', and after winning his place in October 1970, he kept it for the next 7 seasons, mostly wearing the number-9 shirt but operating on the wings, the occasional absence due only to injury. In his first season, he scored in the FA Cup final when Liverpool lost to double-winners Arsenal, and he scored again in the 1974 final, when the Reds beat Newcastle United 3-0. In the 1977 European Cup final victory, against Borussia Mönchengladbach in Rome, he set up the opening goal for Terry McDermott, and then delivered the ball for Tommy Smith to give the Reds a 2-1 lead. It was, though, Kevin Keegan and John Toshack who benefited most from Heighway's impeccable service.

His honours with Liverpool reflected the era in which he played: 4 Football League titles; 1 FA Cup; 1 Football League Cup; 2 European Cups; 2 UEFA Cups; 1 UEFA Super Cup. When he made his final appearance – on 8 April 1981, coming at half-time for McDermott against Bayern Munich in the European Cup semi-final first leg at Anfield – it brought his total of senior games for the Reds to 467 (23 of them as a substitute) with 76 goals scored.

He was due to leave for a new career with Minnesota Kicks in the USA but said, 'I'll be more than happy to stay if I'm needed. It's up to the boss.' Liverpool won the European Cup without him and he was on his way. After Minnesota, Heighway worked for Umbro and Clearwater Chargers before bringing a host of fine players through Liverpool's youth academy. He retired from that position in April 2007, when he was 59.

John Toshack

In November 1970, Liverpool faced an injury crisis. Bobby Graham was nursing a broken ankle, and Ian Callaghan and Alun Evans both had cartilage trouble. They would be out of action for several weeks, if not months. It meant that Bill Shankly's long-standing interest in Cardiff City's 21-year-old striker John Toshack had become a matter of urgency. Then it was announced that Wales would have do without Toshack for their game against Romania in Cardiff. He had twisted an ankle playing against QPR the previous Saturday. Compared to the other injuries, however, that was a minor matter. As the Wales party, minus Toshack, assembled at Ninian Park, Liverpool bid £110,000, Cardiff accepted the offer, the player was happy, and after his flight from Cardiff to Liverpool was cancelled due to a technical problem with the aircraft, he caught a train to Merseyside – Bill Shankly greeted him at the ticket barrier at Lime Street Station – to complete the formalities. Three days later, on 14 November, now fully recovered from his ankle injury, Toshack made his debut for the Reds in a goalless draw at home to Coventry City in what was Peter Thompson's 300th League appearance.

Born in Cardiff on 22 March 1949, Toshack was a Wales schoolboy international when he joined Cardiff City as an apprentice, becoming a full-time professional in March 1966. He had already scored on his League debut when he came off the bench against Leyton Orient, and, a week later, netted twice on his full debut, against Middlesbrough. He was still only 16. He had scored 75 goals in 162 League games for Cardiff when they sold him. The transfer stunned the club's supporters, some of whom never watched the Bluebirds again.

In the week after his move to Anfield, Toshack told the *Liverpool Echo*'s Stan Liversedge:

I accept that if I'm scoring goals, I'm a striker; if not ...
then I'm not much to write home about ... . Those fans at
Anfield know their football – and if you can show them that
you know your stuff, they'll back you through thick and
thin ... . I'm honest enough to admit that the £110,000 price
tag frightens me a little. But I know, too, that I've got to live
with it.

In all, Toshack scored 95 goals in 245 senior appearances (9 as substitute)
for Liverpool, and he made many more, especially for Kevin Keegan
who was the grateful receiver of many a ball nodded on to him by the
big Welshman.

In 1972-73, Toshack made a huge contribution to Liverpool's winning
of the UEFA Cup. The first leg at Anfield, on 9 May, was abandoned after
27 minutes because of a waterlogged pitch. In that time, Shankly had
spotted Borussia Mönchengladbach's big weakness – in the air. When
the game was restaged the following day, he brought in Toshack to
replace the much smaller Brian Hall. After 21 minutes, it was Toshack's
header that set up Keegan's opening goal. Twelve minutes later, from
another Toshack headed knockdown, Keegan made it 2-0. On the hour,
Larry Lloyd made it 3-0 with another header, then Ray Clemence saved
a penalty. Three-nil was enough to take to North-Rhine Westphalia,
where the Reds lost 2-0 to win on aggregate. In 1975-75, Toshack scored
6 goals in the UEFA Cup when Liverpool won it again. That season he
also won his second League championship medal and followed it up
with a third the following year.

Altogether with Liverpool he won 3 League championships,
1 FA Cup, 2 UEFA Cups and a UEFA Super Cup. In 1977, he became
Swansea City's player-manager and took them from the Fourth Division
to the top of the First before the bubble burst. He managed Wales twice,
the first time for only 41 days, the second for 6 years, and also managed
in Spain, Portugal, France, Italy, Morocco, Turkey, Azerbaijan, Iran
and the Macedonian national team, but never returned to Anfield, which
had been his hope. In the 1982 New Year's Honours List he was awarded
the MBE for services to football.

Phil Thompson

That day in August 1969 when he signed as an apprentice for Liverpool would have been a dream come true for Phil Thompson. Born in the Kensington district of the city in January 1954, the third of 7 children, as a schoolboy he stood on the Kop to shout on his favourites. He played for Kirkby Boys and St Joseph's, a Sunday League team, then trained with Everton before Liverpool took him on, and in 1971, the day after his 17th birthday, he became a full-time professional with the Reds.

His League debut came on Easter Monday 1972, in a brilliant 3-0 win at Old Trafford that kept Liverpool in a 4-horse title race with Derby County (the eventual champions), Leeds United and Manchester City. John Toshack had put Liverpool into a 2-0 lead before getting a kick on the side of a leg and limping off, to be replaced by Thompson.

A few weeks later, Thompson played in the Liverpool team beaten by Aston Villa in the FA Youth Cup final. The following season, playing in midfield, he made 14 appearances as Liverpool won the League championship, and had a couple of games in the Reds' successful UEFA Cup campaign. It was 1973-74 when he finally won a regular place, first on the right side of Liverpool's defence before settling down at centre-back as a partner to Emlyn Hughes. Thereafter his gangling figure was a permanent in Liverpool's team for the next 8 seasons. He was a ball-winner but also a skilful footballer whose use of the ball out of defence complemented the 'Crazy Horse' that was Emlyn Hughes.

Thompson played in the 1974 FA Cup final defeat of Newcastle United, but missed Liverpool's first European Cup final win, in 1977, because of injury. In March, near the end of Liverpool's match against Newcastle United at Anfield, he suffered a knee injury which resulted in a cartilage operation that kept him out for the remainder of the season. Thompson had the outer cartilage of his left knee removed. He'd had the inner cartilage removed in September 1974. This latest injury gave another opportunity to Tommy Smith, who had made 6 senior appearances that season.

Thompson was back to play in the winning European Cup teams of 1978 and 1981 to add to the UEFA cup winners' medal that he gained in 1976. Eventually, however, the emergence of Alan Hansen and Mark Lawrenson restricted the number of appearances for Thompson. In December 1984, he went on loan to Sheffield United before making the move permanent in March 1985, retiring at the end of that season. He had made 466 senior appearances (only 7 of them as a substitute) for Liverpool and scored 12 goals. His honours list with Liverpool reads: 7 League championships; 2 European Cups; 1 UEFA Cup; 1 UEFA Super Cup; 1 FA Cup; 2 Football League Cups, together with runners-up medals in all competitions. He made his full England debut against Wales at Wrexham in March 1976, and altogether won 42 caps, skippering his country 6 times. He played in the 1982 World Cup finals in Spain and the 1980 European Championship finals in Italy.

He was still only 31 when he left Sheffield United, but working at a club other than Liverpool was never really going to see Thompson settled and he returned to Anfield to work on the coaching staff under manager Kenny Dalglish. He managed the reserve team before becoming assistant manager to Dalglish and then Graeme Souness until 1992 when there was a falling out. In 1998, he returned as Gérard Houllier's assistant and between October 2001 and March 2002 acted as caretaker manager while Houllier recovered from emergency heart surgery. At the end of that season, Liverpool were runners-up, their best finish in the Premier League.

Today, Thompson works as a football pundit for Sky Sports and occasionally for TV 2 in Norway, and is a regular Visiting Fellow at the University of Liverpool where he teaches on the Football Industries MBA.

Kevin Keegan

'It's fantastic. I'm really delighted. It's a dream come true. I must admit that I was surprised when I heard that Liverpool were after me.' So said 20-year-old Kevin Keegan after he signed for the Reds from Fourth Division Scunthorpe United in May 1971, for £35,000.

Bill Shankly revealed that Liverpool had been watching Keegan for about 9 months. 'We are pleased to have Kevin with us. He's our type of player,' Shankly told the *Liverpool Echo*. 'He's a sturdy little player, very quick and very strong. He knows the game.'

Scunthorpe's season might have been over, but Liverpool still had another game to play – the FA Cup final against Arsenal in 5 days' time. Keegan would travel down to London with his new teammates, to get to know them. He already knew something of Ray Clemence, and had lived in the same Scunthorpe digs as the goalkeeper, although Clemence had moved out a couple of months before Keegan arrived.

Keegan was born at Armthorpe, near Doncaster, on 14 February 1951. Rejected by Coventry City after a trial, he had played in local Doncaster football, with clubs such as Peglar's Brass Works reserves, Elmfield House Youth Club and Lonsdale Hotel FC, before signing for Scunthorpe in 1968. There were only 2,738 spectators to see his final game for the Iron, a 4-0 win over Workington on 1 May 1971, which ensured that Scunthorpe would not have to apply for re-election to the Football League that summer. There were 51,427 to see him mark his First Division debut with the first goal of a 3-1 win over Nottingham Forest on the opening day of the 1971-72 season. It came in front of the Kop after only 12 minutes; 3 minutes later, he was streaking through the Forest defence when Liam O'Kane brought him down and Tommy Smith converted the resultant penalty. 'The New King of Anfield' was the headline in the *Liverpool Echo* as reporter Chris James said:

Like a conjurer out of a hat, Shankly has produced, from nowhere, yet another in the seemingly never-ending stream of young stars coming out of Melwood ... . Keegan showed no sign of nerves on his bow in the First Division and displayed a talent and technique far in advance of his 20 years ... . That he scored on his debut added the icing to the cake, for Keegan, even without that goal, won the hearts of Anfield's demanding crowd.

For a player with speed, the courage to get right into the midst of the action, who could score goals at any level, there was no problem in stepping from the Fourth Division to the First. Over the next 6 seasons there were to be so many highlights – such as Keegan's 2 goals in the 1974 FA Cup final victory over Newcastle United, and the Reds' equaliser in the second leg of the 1976 UEFA Cup final against FC Bruges, which Liverpool won 4-3 on aggregate.

Keegan won 3 League championship winners' medals with Liverpool as well as that FA Cup winners' medal, 2 UEFA Cup winners' medal and a European Cup winners' medal. He was, some might say, a 'self-made' player who rose through dedication as well as skill. That is hard to accept. He was dedicated, of course, but he was also a huge talent who won 63 full caps for England and captained his country 31 times. He was a Footballer of the Year, PFA Player of the Year, and twice a Ballon d'Or winner, and was awarded the OBE in 1982.

In June 1977, after scoring 100 goals in 321 appearances or Liverpool, Keegan was transferred to Hamburger SV for a record Bundesliga fee of £500,000. He won the Bundesliga there before a shock move to Southampton in July 1980, for £400,000, and he then dropped into the Second Division with Newcastle United before retiring in 1984.

Keegan managed Newcastle (twice), Fulham and Manchester City, and had success with all of them, and he managed England from February 1999 to October 2000.

Bob Paisley

Bob Paisley's 30th-minute lob into the Everton goalmouth during the 1950 FA Cup semi-final at Maine Road ended up in the back of the Toffees' net. Billy Liddell jumped for it, so did several Everton defenders, they all missed it and Liverpool were on their way to a 2-0 victory and the final against Arsenal. But when the Wembley team was announced, Paisley, who had played in every Cup match save for the drawn third-round game at Blackburn, was not included. Utility man Bill Jones took his place. Thus, Paisley was denied the opportunity of a unique double: he had won an FA Amateur Cup winners' medal for Bishop Auckland. There were to be plenty of honours ahead for Paisley, some of them not invented when he was playing, but the FA Cup would never be one of them.

The team that lost to Arsenal in the 1950 final included no less than 7 players for whom no transfer fee was paid. Paisley would have made 8. Born in Hetton-le-Hole in County Durham on 23 January 1919, he joined Liverpool from Bishop Auckland in May 1939, just after their FA Amateur final defeat of neighbours Willington at Roker Park. During the Second World War, he served in the Army and guested for Bristol City, making his League debut for Liverpool on 7 September 1946, against Chelsea at Anfield in the third game of a season that saw the Reds win the first post-war League championship. Paisley played 33 times.

A powerful, all-action wing-half, he was a regular member of the side – apart from the odd Cup final, and in 1949-50 when he missed half the season after injuring a knee against Middlesbrough in October – until well into the 1950s. When he retired in 1954, Paisley had made 278 appearances, scored 13 goals and created several more with his long throw-ins. He joined the Anfield backroom staff, first as assistant trainer, then chief trainer in 1957, and was Bill Shankly's assistant for many years before being appointed manager in July 1974, after Shankly retired. Unlike Shankly, Paisley kept a low profile. For him, the football did the talking.

And talk it did.

Bob Paisley became one of the most successful managers in the history of English football, winning for Liverpool 6 League championships, 3 European Cups, 1 UEFA Cup and 3 Football League Cups. He played the masterstroke of moving Ray Kennedy from striker to midfield, and signed Kenny Dalglish and Graeme Souness, both of whom were to follow in his footsteps and manage Liverpool. His signings, such as Terry McDermott, Phil Neal and Joey Jones, prospered while young men from the Melwood production line – the likes of Jimmy Case and David Fairclough – rose to fame. A fine team was strengthened still further and if his first season in charge brought no honours, every season after that brought them in abundance.

When Liverpool won the First Division in 1975-76, they needed victory at Molineux to clinch the title. Paisley's mind perhaps went back to May 1947, when to become champions the Reds also needed to win at Wolves. They won 2-1; in 1976 they won 3-1. Paisley took the team that he inherited from Shankly and maintained them as one of the world's greatest club sides. The 1978-79 League championship was probably the most remarkable of all Liverpool's achievements under Bob Paisley. They conceded only 16 goals in their League matches, only 4 of them at Anfield, with goalkeeper Ray Clemence keeping a record 28 clean sheets. Thirty wins and only 4 defeats gave them a record 68 points from a 42-match First Division season when only 2 points were awarded for a win.

Paisley was awarded the OBE in 1977 and voted Manager of the Year a record 6 times. After he decided to retire in June 1983, he remained as an advisor to his successors and also served on the board until resigning through ill-health in February 1992. He died on 14 February 1996, aged 77, after suffering from Alzheimer's disease for some years.

Phil Neal

On Wednesday, 9 October 1974. Northampton Town defender Phil Neal travelled up to Anfield with the Cobblers' manager, Dave Bowen, and after a successful medical examination the deal was done, for £60,000.

Bob Paisley told Michael Charters of the *Liverpool Echo*:

> I have had 5 separate reports on Neal, some from our own staff, and others from influential men whose judgement I respect. They have all confirmed that Neal is the type of player – still young but with plenty of League experience – that I have been looking for as defensive cover. We have transferred two centre-halves this season. Larry Lloyd forced himself away and Dave Rylands went because we could see no first-team opportunity for him at Anfield.

The Liverpool manager pointed out that he had never been able to field a full-strength team in any match so far that season, and injury had also played a part in him having to look for new players: 'When we first had reports on Neal, he was playing at full-back and looking good, and then he was switched to centre-half and did well there. He is a 6-footer, well built, and I am sure he will provide the additional cover in defence that I want.'

Neal would do much more than that. He turned out to be one of the most important signings that Paisley would ever make. A 23-year-old veteran of 187 Third and Fourth Division appearances for Northampton Town, Neal was given his First Division debut against Everton at Goodison Park on 16 November 1974. He missed the next 3 matches but then played in every game to the season's end. From the start of 1975-76, he was ever-present for the next 8 seasons, and altogether missed only 1 League match in 10 seasons. He liked to overlap, which, together with the fact that he was one of the most reliable penalty-takers in the game, resulted in the remarkable – for a full-back – total of 60 goals that he scored in his 635 appearances for Liverpool, only 2 of which were as a substitute. Twice he might have had that sequence broken: when he suffered a broken nose; and when for several weeks he managed with a broken toe in plaster while wearing a bigger-sized boot over that foot.

Neal, who was born in the Northamptonshire village of Irchester on 20 February 1951, played with his local club and for Wellingborough Town before joining Northampton Town as an apprentice in July 1967, signing as a full-time professional in December 1968.

His honours with Liverpool comprised 7 League championships (he made only 11 full appearances when the title was won again in 1985-86), 4 European Cups, 1 UEFA Cup, 1 UEFA Super Cup and 4 League Cups. He captained the Reds and was the only player to have appeared in those first 4 European Cup final victories. One of the goals in the 3-1 win over Borussia Mönchengladbach in the 1977 final was an 82nd-minute penalty scored by Neal, and he also scored from the spot in the 1984 penalty shootout against AS Roma after Steve Nicol had missed the Reds' first attempt.

He made his full England debut in March 1976, against Wales at Wrexham, alongside Phil Thompson, Kevin Keegan and Ray Kennedy, and his 50th and final appearance came against Denmark at Wembley in September 1983.

In December 1985, after 11 years at Anfield, Neal left to become player-manager of Bolton Wanderers, who were then in the Third Division. He remained at Burnden Park for 7 years, although during that time the Trotters were relegated – they were promoted the following season – and the only trophy they won during Neal's tenure was the Football League trophy. When he retired as a player in 1989, Neal had taken his total of senior matches in English football to over 900. He left Bolton in 1992 and was later England manager Graham Taylor's assistant, and then managed Coventry City and Cardiff City, and was assistant manager and caretaker manager at Manchester City and assistant manager at Peterborough United.

Terry McDermott

It was a roundabout journey that brought Terry McDermott back to his native Merseyside, and longer still before he won a regular place in the Liverpool first team. But, after he did, he won a rich collection of honours at Anfield.

Born in Kirkby on 8 December 1951, after starring in Liverpool schools' football McDermott joined Bury as an apprentice before turning full-time professional in October 1969. He made 101 appearances and scored 10 goals for the Shakers before Newcastle United bought him for £22,000 in February 1973, after an on-off-on deal about which his mother, Margaret, told the (*Newcastle) Evening Chronicle*: 'My husband and I are all in favour of Terry going to Newcastle – and we'll be telling him so.' Bury manager Allan Brown agreed: 'It's in the player's own best interests to join a First Division club.' Bury were then in the Fourth Division.

And so the 21-year-old McDermott, who despite his slight build was an aggressive midfielder, signed for Newcastle. He turned out to be one of manager Joe Harvey's best buys, but it was a clash with Harvey that saw him leave St James's Park, for Anfield in November 1974, for £170,000. Six months earlier he had been Newcastle's man of the match when they lost the FA Cup final to Liverpool. In September, however, he had still not re-signed for the Magpies, and it was only ever going to end one way – McDermott had his wish and Liverpool had a player who would give them splendid service with his penetrating runs from midfield and some spectacular goals.

At first McDermott struggled to make an impression, and Bob Paisley kept him under wraps. It was 1977-78 before he established himself in the first team. The previous season, when he made 25 starts in the First Division, he returned to Wembley when Liverpool met Manchester United in the FA Cup final. He was on the losing side again that day, but when the Reds met Borussia Mönchengladbach in the 1977 European Cup final in Rome, he scored their first goal. It came after 28 minutes when McDermott took Heighway's inch-perfect pass to clip the ball wide of Wolfgang Kneib in the German club's goal.

Another European Cup medal followed the next year, against Club Bruges at Wembley, and yet another in 1981 when Real Madrid were beaten in Paris. Besides those 3 European medals, McDermott also won 4 League championship medals and 2 League Cup medals. His goal against Everton in the 1977 FA Cup semi-final against Everton at Maine Road – a brilliant chip from the edge of the penalty area – was the BBC TV's 'goal of the season'. In September 1978, when Spurs were thrashed 7-0, after starting the move, McDermott ran 60 yards to head home Steve Heighway's cross. Bob Paisley said it was 'the best goal seen at Anfield for 60 years'.

McDermott made his full England debut in September 1977, against Switzerland at Wembley. He played in the 1980 European championships in Italy and altogether won 25 caps and scored 3 goals for England. In 1980, he was voted Footballer of the Year and also PFA Player of the Year.

McDermott played his last game for Liverpool in September 1982, against Dundalk in the European Cup. He already knew that he was returning to Newcastle after another on-off transfer. The club had agreed a fee of £100,000 but the Magpies could not initially agree terms with the player. Once sorted, McDermott said, 'I haven't had a full game for Liverpool since the beginning of April … . I've really enjoyed my time here and to know you're playing your last game is uncanny.' He had scored 75 goals in 322 (12 as substitute) games for Liverpool.

He played in another 74 League games for Newcastle, scoring 12 goals, before leaving again 2 years later. He retired from playing after spells with Cork City and Apoel Nicosia. He coached at Newcastle under, among others, Keegan, Dalglish and Souness, and was assistant manager at Huddersfield Town and Birmingham City.

Jimmy Case

Jimmy Case was one of the last of an era – a local boy who learned his football with players older and bigger than himself; a young man who continued a trade apprenticeship even after he was playing for the reserve team of a top-flight club. It was an upbringing and introduction to the full-time professional League game that never gave a player a sense of entitlement, and ensured that he always knew how privileged he was to be doing something of which most boys only ever dreamed.

Jimmy Case was born in Liverpool on 18 May 1954, and grew up on the Allerton council estate that was home to Paul McCartney before the world had heard of The Beatles. Small for his age, Case joined a team called the Blue Union, a name that will resonate with anyone who knows about the Merseyside dockers who defended their rights in the 1950s. The football team was full of tough dockers, and the physical nature of their play would define Jimmy Case's football career. He was small in stature but he quickly learned to hold his own in midfield and up front.

After leaving school, Case trained to become an electrician and played for Northern Premier League club South Liverpool. A cartilage operation in September 1971 could not hold him back and the following March, aged 17, he made his first-team debut for them. In September 1972, he gave up his 2 weeks' annual holiday to train full-time with Liverpool at Melwood. He signed amateur forms for the Reds, and in April 1973, he made his Central League debut for them. The following month he signed professional forms, South Liverpool receiving £500 in exchange for losing their star teenager.

Case made his League debut in the last match of the 1974-75 season, at home to QPR. In the *Liverpool Echo*, Michael Charters wrote, 'I've no doubt that the happiest player on the pitch was Jimmy Case, who showed immense promise in his first senior game and played with such ability and sense that he must be in line for a regular place next season. He was involved in all 3 Liverpool goals.'

Case made 27 League starts in 1975-76, 30 in 1977-78, and missed only 10 League games in the next 2 seasons. He was the classic type of inside-forward, as his position was known in those days, industrious and possessing a powerful shot, so much so that he became entrusted with any free-kick that was considered within shooting range. His right-foot volleyed equaliser against Manchester United in the 1977 FA Cup final – albeit, Liverpool lost – was typical. He scored in the first leg of the 1976 UEFA Cup final against Club Bruges at Anfield, and altogether played in 4 League championship-winning teams and in 3 winning European Cup final teams.

After Case and teammate Ray Kennedy were each fined £150 for assaulting 2 men at a North Wales hotel, Bob Paisley recognised that Case's fame and his local connections – there were always several drinks lined up for him by appreciative supporters – might prove an ongoing problem. In August 1981 he was transferred to Brighton and Hove Albion for a fee reported to be around £350,000. Mark Lawrenson came the other way, valued at £900,00 with Case the 'makeweight'. In February 1983, Case returned to Anfield with the Seasiders and scored the winning goal in the fifth round of the FA Cup, a 70th-minute a right-foot volley that was deflected into the net and which sent Brighton into the quarter-finals for the first time in their history. Brighton reached Wembley that season, where they drew 2-2 with Manchester United before losing the replay 4-0. In March 1985, Case was transferred to Southampton for £25,000. He later played for Harry's Redknapp's Bournemouth, then for Halifax Town, Wrexham and Brighton again, a club he managed for a short while. He later managed non-League Bashley, and then summarised Liverpool matches on BBC Radio Merseyside. He made 261 appearances (25 as substitute) for Liverpool and scored 45 goals for the Reds.

David Fairclough

Saturday, 3 April 1976 was Grand National day and so the Merseyside derby at Anfield kicked off early. The race was won by 14/1 shot Rag Trade, who beat the favourite, Red Rum, into second place. The big match headline in that afternoon's *Liverpool Echo* was, 'Super Sub Does It Again!'

There were 2 minutes remaining when David Fairclough won the ball in the Everton half, left several opponents in his wake, reached the penalty area and unleashed a right-foot drive that flew past Blues' goalkeeper Dai Davies and into the corner of the net. It was the only goal of the game – moments later, Phil Neal missed a penalty for Liverpool for the first time after Bryan Hamilton handled a Keegan shot.

Fairclough had come on as a 64th-minute substitute for John Toshack. He told the *Echo*'s Alex Goodman, 'I just did what comes naturally to me … when I was sitting on the bench there seemed to be plenty of chances about … when I came on, I decided to get my share.' In the previous 2 League matches, Fairclough scored the only goal of the game at Norwich City, and both goals in a 2-0 win over Burnley at Anfield – so all the goals in victories that kept Liverpool on track for the First Division title. Bob Paisley joked, 'I would have entered him for the Grand National, had it been possible – he'd have won that as well.'

Fast forward to 16 March 1977. Liverpool are drawing 2-2 on aggregate against Saint-Etienne in the European Cup quarter-final second leg at Anfield. Eighteen minutes from the end of normal time, Fairclough again comes on for the injured Toshack. Twelve minutes later, from a Ray Clemence clearance, Ray Kennedy slips the ball through to Fairclough who holds off a challenge from Christian Lopez, draws Ivan Ćurković out of goal, and then strokes the ball home at the Kop end. The noise is deafening. Six minutes later, Dutch referee Charles Corver

138

sounds the final whistle. Liverpool win 3-2 over the 2 games. Super Sub has done it yet again.

It was an inevitable sobriquet, but one that Fairclough neither liked nor appreciated. Altogether he made 149 senior appearances for Liverpool – and 61 of them were as a substitute. Of his 52 goals, only 15 came as a substitute, leaving 37 from 88 starts, which is a handsome strike rate in itself. It seemed that whenever he played – full games or parts of games – he was always likely to find goal. Thirty-four of his League goals came in 64 starts. Again, it is a percentage with which any striker would be pleased. Yet his goals when he came on as a replacement were generally the headline-grabbers. We must not forget, though, his hat-trick in the 5-3 thriller at Carrow Road in February 1980. They came in the fourth, 18th and 75th minute. Dalglish (88) and Case (89) finished the job.

David Fairclough was born close to Anfield on 5 January 1957. He joined Liverpool as a junior, signing full-time professional forms in January 1974. With his red hair and his dazzling runs, he was always going to catch the eye, although some said that he sometimes drifted out of matches. He did more than enough, though, to be one of the most memorable players of his era.

He felt that Paisley might have started with him more often, and perhaps that is why the 'Super Sub' tag rankled. He played in the 1978 European Cup final win, in the 1976 UEFA Cup final victory, in the winning 1977 UEFA Super Cup team and in the side that won the 1983 Football League Cup. He also played in a handful of games in each of the League championship-winning seasons of 1975-76, 1976-77, 1978-79 and 1979-80. His last appearance for Liverpool was in April 1983, after a spell with Toronto Blizzard. Then he played for Lucerne, Norwich City, Oldham Athletic, Beveren, Tranmere Rovers and Wigan Athletic where he ended his playing career in 1990-91.

Graeme Souness

On 2 January 1978, Middlesbrough announced that their midfield star Graeme Souness had been suspended for a week for a breach of club discipline (the reason for which the manager refused to divulge). The previous month, before the European Cup quarter-final deadline of 16 December, Middlesbrough had turned down a £325,000 bid from the Reds for the unsettled Souness.

On 11 January, Liverpool had their man. Souness signed for Liverpool with Boro receiving £352,000, a record between Football League clubs. The 24-year-old said, 'I realised that Middlesbrough would never become a Liverpool in my career. I wanted to go to a club where I was going to win something. Now I hope that Liverpool get through to the quarter-finals of the European Cup, so that I'm eligible to play in the semi-finals.' By the end of the season, he was the holder of a European Cup winners' medal after supplying the pass from which Kenny Dalglish scored the only goal of the game, in the 64th minute, against Club Bruges at Wembley.

Although sometimes described as 'over-robust', Souness was an elegant player with great vision and wonderful ball control, allied to a fierce shot. Born in Edinburgh on 6 May 1953, he joined Spurs as an apprentice in April 1969, becoming a full-time professional in May the following year. Frustrated by a lack of first-team opportunities at White Hart Lane, after a summer spent in the NASL with Montreal Olympique, in January 1973 he moved to Middlesbrough for £32,000. Capped by Scotland under-23s in his first season at Ayresome Park, he helped Boro win promotion from the Second Division in 1974. But, as he said, they never looked likely to compete for top honours, and after 204 appearances and 23 goals for them, he was on his way to Anfield. He won the first of his 54 full caps for Scotland while still with Middlesbrough.

With Liverpool, the honours flowed his way: 5 League championships; 3 European Cups; 3 Football League Cups. After scoring in the penalty shootout that gave Liverpool the 1984 European Cup final against AS Roma, Souness said, 'They say the penalty shootout was dramatic television but imagine playing another half-hour or an hour on top of games like that one. It would be really exciting … players would be dropping like flies. You would certainly get a result before midnight.'

A few days later, commenting on rumours that he was moving to Italian football, he said, 'I'll still be here next season.' The same month, however, he signed for Sampdoria in a £650,000 transfer. He had made 350 starts (and 2 substitute appearances) and scored 56 goals for Liverpool. In 1986 he joined Rangers, winning the Scottish Premier Division once as a player-manager and twice as manager before, in April 1991, Liverpool appointed him to succeed Kenny Dalglish who had resigned. Faced with an ageing team, Souness won only the FA Cup, in 1992, for the Reds and was criticised for clearing out too many players to quickly – although in his first 12 months it was not as dramatic an overhaul as has sometimes been suggested – and then replacing them with lesser performers. Supporters who had welcomed his appointment began to question it.

There was also the interview that Souness gave to *The Sun* – a newspaper reviled on Merseyside after its scandalous reporting of the Hillsborough tragedy – concerning his heart bypass operation. It was to be published alongside a report of the 1992 FA Cup semi-final replay against Portsmouth, but the game went to extra-time and the deadline was missed. Instead, the article appeared on the third anniversary of the day on which 95 fans died (another would die the following year, having never regained consciousness). Souness's status was now that of fallen hero from which it was hard to recover. In January 1994, after Liverpool lost an FA Cup third-round tie at home to second-tier Bristol City, he stepped down as Liverpool manager. He later managed Galatasaray, Southampton, Torino, Benfica, Blackburn Rovers and Newcastle United, and is today a well-known analyst on Sky Sports.

Alan Hansen

On 5 May 1977, Liverpool manager Bob Paisley completed a transfer that had been bubbling for ages, when 21-year-old Scotland under-23 centre-back Alan Hansen sign for the Reds from Scottish Premier Division club Partick Thistle. Liverpool and Partick had agreed terms a week earlier, and the player was happy to move to Merseyside, but Paisley was looking forward. Hansen would have been ineligible to play for Liverpool in the closing stages of their First Division title-winning race, and so the Liverpool boss decided to leave him to play out the season with his first professional club.

Paisley told the *Liverpool Echo*'s Michael Charters that he had bought Hansen for the same reason that he had moved for Northampton Town defender Phil Neal, 3 years earlier: as cover for more than just a single position. 'The all-purpose player, particularly at the back, is a growing trend in the modern game,' said Paisley. 'I've seen Hansen play and he's not only a strong defender, but he can play football as well. He's not just a stopper.'

Paisley promised to bring along Hansen slowly, just as Liverpool had done with Clemence, Kennedy, McDermott, Jones and Neal: 'He'll learn the Anfield way in the reserves – you have your successes and everything's great … but you still have to think about the future of the team and try to maintain the blend which is vital.'

Hansen was born in Sauchie, Clackmannanshire, on 13 June 1955. He joined Partick from Sauchie Juniors in July 1972, and at the time of signing for Liverpool still lived in the village, 1 mile from Alloa. All that was about to change. He told Charters:

> I couldn't be making a better move. Liverpool are the best
> in the business and they've proved that for years. It's going
> to be great for me to mix with these great players just when

they're about to win their championship and are into the finals of the FA and European Cups. I was looked on as one of the stars at Partick but I realise that I'm just about to start my real football education.

He could have added that not only was he a versatile footballer, he was also an accomplished all-round sportsman, winning junior representative honours at squash, volleyball and golf.

Hansen made his League debut for Liverpool in September 1977, in a 1-0 home win over Derby County. As Paisley had described, he was an elegant defender, and by the following season was a regular in the number-6 shirt in Liverpool's first team. Like David Fairclough, he was an eye-catching footballer, but for totally different reasons. Not only did he possess superb close control, but his positional sense was also outstanding. He won 26 full caps for Scotland, and with Liverpool played in the European Cup finals of 1978, 1981 and 1984, all won, and in the awful 1985 final in Brussels, a game forever known for the Heysel disaster. He played in no less than 8 League championship-winning seasons for the Reds, 2 winning FA Cup final teams, 4 Football League Cup final victories and a UEFA Super Cup win.

In 1988-89 he missed much of the season due to a knee injury but was recalled for the FA Cup semi-final against Nottingham Forest and thus appeared in the game at Hillsborough, a match that was abandoned after only 6 minutes in unbelievably tragic circumstances. That season, due to Hansen's absence, Ronnie Whelan took over the Liverpool captaincy, and although Hansen played in the emotionally charged FA Cup final, it was Whelan who collected the trophy after the Reds' 3-2 extra-time victory over Everton.

Although Hansen played in 31 games when Liverpool won the League championship in 1989-90, it was his last season. He was in his mid-30s and injuries had taken their toll. He announced his retirement in March 1991, soon after Kenny Dalglish resigned as manager. Hansen had made 603 starts and 4 substitute appearances and scored 13 goals for Liverpool. He turned down opportunities to coach and instead became a respected football analyst for BBC TV.

Sammy Lee

Sammy Lee made an instant impression on his League debut for Liverpool, on 8 April 1978, at home to Leicester City. Coming on as a seventh-minute substitute for David Johnson, who limped off with a knee injury, Lee marked his first appearance with a goal. Bottom-of-the-table Leicester twice took the lead against the championship-chasing Reds before Tommy Smith scored his second goal of the game to give Liverpool a 3-2 win. The second equaliser, though, belonged to 19-year-old Lee, when Leicester goalkeeper Mark Wallington let a 20-yard shot through his legs. It was a howler, but Lee celebrated in style – and who could have blamed him?

Sammy Lee was born in Liverpool on 7 February 1959. He joined Liverpool as a junior and signed full-time professional forms in 1976. Despite that goalscoring debut, it was 1980-81 before he became an established member of the team. All the many honours he won with Liverpool came in the first half of that decade.

Of small stature but strong, Lee was, according to older Liverpool supporters, in the Bob Paisley mould; a busy midfielder who won the ball, used it well, and never seemed to stop running from August until May. He was a key player in all of Liverpool's triumphs before injury and loss of form hit him in 1985-86.

With the Reds, he won 4 League championships – the hat-trick seasons of 1981-2, 1982-83 and 1983-84, and he also appeared 15 times in the 1985-86 win – and played in the winning European Cup final teams of 1981 and 1984. In the 1981 European Cup semi-final, against Bayern Munich, it was Lee's man-marking of Paul Breitner that, as much as anything, saw Liverpool through to the final against Real Madrid.

There were also Football League Cup final medals as Liverpool won the trophy 4 times in succession between 1981 and 1984. In the 1981 final against West Ham United at Wembley, Lee played a controversial, albeit unwitting, part in Alan Kennedy's goal. He was lying injured in an offside position – the law was less liberal than it is today – when Kennedy followed up to score the first goal of the game, which was now well into extra-time. A linesman flagged but, much to the Hammers' chagrin, referee Clive Thomas allowed the goal to stand. Earlier, Lee had the ball in the net off a post but on that occasion Colin Irwin was adjudged to have strayed offside. Although West Ham managed an equaliser, Liverpool won the replay, 2-1 at Villa Park.

In November 1982, Bobby Robson awarded Lee the first of 14 full caps for England when the Liverpool man was selected to play against Greece in a European championship qualifier in Thessalonica. Just like his League debut for Liverpool, Lee scored in his first international match as England won 3-0. He also scored against Hungary in Budapest in October 1983, in another 3-0 win.

By 1985, Lee, still only 26, was becoming increasingly troubled by injury, and Jan Molby was now first choice. In August 1986, Lee was transferred to QPR for £200,000. For Liverpool, he had played in 286 senior games (only 7 as a substitute) and scored 19 goals. He played in 30 League matches for QPR before moving to Spain to play with Osasuna, for 3 La Liga seasons, and he ended his playing career with a few games each for Southampton and Bolton Wanderers.

He returned to Anfield – where Graeme Souness was now manager – to work as a coach, a role he continued under Ray Evans and Gérard Houllier before becoming part of the England coaching staff under Sven-Göran Eriksson. A spell as Sam Allardyce's assistant at Bolton Wanderers was followed by a short and frenetic spell –170 days, 14 games, only 3 victories but 12 signings – as the Trotters' manager. Then he was back at Anfield as Rafael Benitez's assistant before coaching and assistant (or caretaker) manager's jobs back at Bolton, then Southampton, England again, Crystal Palace and Everton, most of them under Allardyce again.

Mark Lawrenson

In August 1981, Brighton's Irish international centre-back, Mark Lawrenson, now a free agent, was talking to Arsenal who were keen to sign him after David O'Leary had missed much of the previous season with a damaged heel. Terms had been agreed between the Seagulls and the Gunners, but the Liverpool chairman, John Smith, told the *Liverpool Echo*, 'We are always in the hunt for good players – and Lawrenson is a good player.' If Liverpool did sign Lawrenson, then they would have to smash the club record fee of £650,000 they had paid Middlesbrough for Craig Johnston the previous April.

A few days later, Lawrenson was a Liverpool player for a £900,000 transfer fee – provided he wanted to join them. The Reds were at the end of a pre-season 3-match trip to Switzerland, which meant a difficult few days for chairman Smith and manager Bob Paisley. Communication was not so easy in those times – no mobile telephones or emails to ease things along. While the rest of the Liverpool party flew on to Merseyside from Heathrow, Smith and Paisley were meeting Lawrenson in a London hotel to discuss personal terms.

At the end of that day, 3 men – Smith, Paisley and Lawrenson – were back home. Lawrenson knew the north west well; he was born in Preston on 2 June 1957, and had started his career at Preston North End before signing for Brighton for £100,000 in 1977. Even better, his mother and stepfather lived at Lytham St Annes, so after completing all the documents at Anfield, he could pop over to see them and, at the same time, deliver his own transfer papers to the nearby Football League headquarters.

Brighton had never wanted to sell him but, faced with financial problems, they had little choice. At the Goldstone Ground, Lawrenson had blossomed into a versatile defender, one of the best in the First Division. Ironically, Brighton had originally outbid Liverpool to get him from Preston. After he played against the Reds for Brighton, and managed to take the ball off Kenny Dalglish, Paisley was not prepared to let him escape a second time.

Lawrenson had helped Brighton into the First Division in 1979, and now he was on the brink of a new career that would bring him so many top honours. From the moment he made his Liverpool debut, on 29 August 1981 – a less than memorable 1-0 defeat at Wolves – he was virtually an ever-present. At the end of his first season, he had a League championship medal, and again the following season and another the season after that – and yet again in 1985-86 and 1987-88, albeit by the latter season he played only 14 times. There was a European Cup winners' medal in 1984, an FA Cup winners' medal in 1986, and Football League Cup winners' medals in 1982, 1983 and 1984. He won a total of 39 Republic of Ireland caps – although born in England he qualified through his mother – and 24 of those came as a Liverpool player.

He began his Liverpool career at left-back before moving into the centre of defence. He would play 341 times for the Reds, 9 of them coming off the bench, and score 17 goals, sometimes quite important ones such as the 53rd -minute headed equaliser he put past Tottenham's Ray Clemence in the penultimate match of 1981-82. It set the Reds on the road to a 3-1 win at Anfield, a result that clinched the League championship. He also set up Liverpool's second goal for Dalglish, hooking the ball over his head for Dalglish to dummy Clemence before slipping it into the net.

In March 1988, Lawrenson left Anfield for the Manor Ground at Oxford, where he became manager, a job that lasted only 7 months and ended when he became exasperated that Robert Maxwell had let star striker Dean Saunders go to Derby County. There followed jobs with Barnet, Tampa Bay, Peterborough United and Newcastle United, and some games for Corby Town and Chesham United before Lawrenson became part of the BBC TV *Match of the Day* team.

Kenny Dalglish

Bob Paisley knew exactly what he was getting when Liverpool paid £440,000 – a record transfer fee between British clubs – to sign Kenny Dalglish from Celtic in August 1977. Paisley was looking for a replacement for Kevin Keegan, who that summer had been sold to Hamburger SV for £500,000.

Dalglish had already won 47 caps for Scotland and scored more than 100 goals for Celtic. It was no secret that he had become unsettled at Parkhead, opting out of Celtic's pre-season trip to Hong Kong and Australia. Paisley said, 'We have signed a very talented player. Kenny will do a great job for us.'

Dalglish would have an enormous impact on Liverpool. He scored in the seventh minute of his League debut, against Middlesbrough at Ayresome Park. That season he was ever-present in the League, scored 20 goals from those 42 matches, and finished it all off with the winning goal in the European Cup final against FC Bruges at Wembley. It was the only 1 of the game, and what a peach of a goal it was. It came in the 65th minute when he ran on to a through ball from Graeme Souness, went clear, and then, not so much shot but passed the ball into the net. By the end of 1985-86 he had more than doubled his number of caps – he ended with a record 102 full appearances – and was the first player to score a century of League goals in both Scotland and England. He was a rare talent.

It did not stop there. When Joe Fagan retired as Liverpool's manager in 1985, Dalglish accepted the job of player-manager. It was the first time the club had made such an appointment. There were more than a few raised eyebrows at Anfield, but, in his first season in the role, Dalglish took Liverpool to the League and FA Cup double. He was Manager of the Year that season, and again in 1988 and 1990 before resigning in 1991. His final appearance had come on 5 May 1990, as a substitute at home to Derby County, when he was 39 (he was born in Glasgow on 4 March 1951). It was the last of 497 senior appearances for Liverpool (16 as a sub) in which he had scored 168 goals. Altogether with Liverpool he won 8 League championships, 3 European Cups, 2 FA Cups, 5 Football League Cups and 1 UEFA Super Cup. At times under his management Liverpool seemed almost unbeatable, and in part of 1987-88 they conceded only 1 goal in 15 matches in all competitions.

In February 1991, Dalglish resigned as Liverpool's manager, citing 'pressure of work'. The football world was stunned. At the time of his resignation, Liverpool were still in the FA Cup and topped the First Division by 3 points. The following day they crashed 3-1 on Luton Town's artificial pitch and ended the season as runners-up, 7 points behind Arsenal.

In October 1991, Dalglish returned to management with Blackburn Rovers. At Ewood Park he wove his magic again, taking Blackburn from the Second Division to the Premier League title with the help of record signings Alan Shearer and Chris Sutton. He then managed Newcastle United and Celtic before returning to Anfield in 2009 as academy director. In January 2011, he became caretaker manager when Roy Hodgson left, then took the job permanently, in 2011-12 leading Liverpool to the Football League Cup, their first trophy for 6 years. But they lost that season's FA Cup final and could finish only eighth in the table, their lowest final placing since 1994. Dalglish left again, but returned once more, this time as a non-executive director, in 2017. In 1984 he was awarded the MBE, and in 2018 he was knighted in recognition of his contributions both on and off the football field, including working with families affected by the Hillsborough disaster, and also the charity that he and his wife, Marina, set up and which had so far raised more than £10 million to help treat cancer.

Alan Kennedy

Newcastle United defender Alan Kennedy had 1 overriding priority to settle before he could agree to sign for Liverpool. In August 1978, the clubs had agreed the fee – £330,000 – but the player had some personal business. Three months earlier, his mother had died, and Kennedy felt that his widowed father might want his son to remain close to him in the north east. Only when Kennedy senior gave his approval of the move did the transfer go through. Kennedy had already flown to Vienna, where the Reds were playing a pre-season friendly, to talk with Bob Paisley, but he wanted to be certain that everything was right on the domestic front. That established, the forms were signed in a Liverpool hotel and everyone could move forward.

Although he had been with Newcastle since joining them as an apprentice in July 1971, Kennedy was born in Sunderland, on 31 August 1954. He had won England under-23 and B caps, and been selected for the full side in 1975 but a knee injury prevented his appearance. The previous year, after only a handful of first-team games, he had played in the FA Cup final defeat by Liverpool. An attacking full-back, he had made 194 appearances and scored 9 goals for the Magpies before joining Liverpool. His elder brother, Keith, had also been on Newcastle's books but now played for Bury, so there was family in Lancashire already.

Kennedy made his debut against Celtic in Jock Stein's testimonial match at Parkhead, a game watched by 60,000 fans. His League bow for the Reds came in the opening game of the season, against QPR at Anfield. Liverpool won 2-1 and Kennedy laid on the opening goal for Kenny Dalglish, taking a pass from Steve Heighway before delivering it for Dalglish to finish off. That apart, it was not the most impressive debut and he later recalled that Paisley told him, 'I think they shot the wrong Kennedy.'

At left-back he took over Joey Jones, who was about to be transferred back to his first club, Wrexham, and missed only 10 League matches in the next 2 seasons. In September 1980, Kennedy injured an ankle against Birmingham City at St Andrew's but remained on the field because Liverpool had already used their substitute when David Johnson was injured. That and other knocks, including a hamstring strain and a knee injury, kept him out for large parts of the season – he made only 19 starts in the League – but it was his 81st-minute goal that won the 1981 European Cup final against Real Madrid. Another vital European Cup final goal came in the 1984 penalty shootout against Roma. There was also the 75th-minute equaliser in the 1983 League Cup final against Manchester United.

Back to full fitness, Kennedy missed only 20 out of 168 League games between 1981-82 and 1984-85, and in April 1984 he finally won the England cap that injury had denied him 9 years earlier. He played against Northern Ireland at Wembley and was capped again the following month, against Wales at Wrexham.

In September 1985, he was transferred to his hometown club, Sunderland, for £100,000. Jim Beglin had taken over the left-back role and it was cruel that Kennedy's final appearance, at Oxford United on 14 September, should be best remembered for his own-goal that cost Liverpool a victory. They drew 2-2. It was also Steve McMahon's first game after his £350,000 move from Aston Villa.

Alan Kennedy had made 349 appearances for Liverpool (including 2 as a substitute) and scored 21 goals. He had 5 League championship winners' medals, 2 European Cup winners' medals, 1 FA Cup and 4 Football League Cup winners' medals.

After Sunderland, for whom he made 54 League appearances, Kennedy played briefly for both Hartlepool United and Beerschot (Belgium), had trials with the Swedish club Husqvarna FF and then Boldklubben 1903 in Copenhagen. Returning to England, he turned out for Northwich Victoria, Grantham Town, Wigan Athletic, Colne Dynamoes, Wrexham, Morecambe, Netherfield, Radcliffe Borough and Barrow before retiring when he was 42.

Ian Rush

In May 1980, Liverpool paid £300,000 for a 19-year-old striker who had scored 17 goals in 39 first-team appearances for Chester, who needed the money to help pay for their new stand at Sealand Road. Bob Paisley explained, 'I've watched him play a couple of times ... . He's got a lot of potential and I think that he's a good buy for us, a lad for the future.'

Ian Rush started the 1980-81 season in the reserves and by mid-December had scored 10 goals in 16 Central League matches. Then Kenny Dalglish injured an ankle, and Rush was given his First Division debut against championship rivals Ipswich Town at Portman Road. It was a big responsibility – Dalglish had not missed a Liverpool game for 3 years.

Paisley confessed that introducing Rush had not been an easy decision to make. He told the *Liverpool Echo*, 'What swayed it in the end was the thought that it would best to replace a striker with a striker. If we'd picked anyone else it would have meant playing them out of position.'

The game ended 1-1, and, like the rest of his teammates, Rush was never able to get going against Bobby Robson's side. It was a stuttering start for the boy from St Asaph, but, even so, his second senior game was no less than the Football League Cup final replay against West Ham at Villa Park when he hit the woodwork with a shot. By the end of the season, his 9 games for the Reds – he also played in the first leg of the European Cup semi-final against Bayern Munich – had still not produced a goal.

On 30 September 1981, he finally found 1, coming on as a substitute and scoring 1 of Liverpool's 7 in the European Cup hammering of Finnish club, Oulu Palloseura. Thereafter, Rush could not stop scoring and over the next 6 seasons would become the greatest striker in Liverpool's history. He ended 1981-82 as top scorer with 30 goals, winning a League championship medal and scoring in Liverpool's League Cup final win over Tottenham. When the League title was retained in 1982-83, he scored 4 in a 5-0 win at Goodison Park, and 3 against Coventry the following week. In 1983-84, as Liverpool won the First Division yet again, his 48 goals in all competitions included 5 at home to Luton and another 4 at home to Coventry.

It was the European ban on English clubs after the Heysel tragedy that saw Liverpool forced to sell their star striker, to Juventus for a British record fee of £3.2 million, in the summer of 1986; although after Michel Platini decided to play another season, Rush was loaned back to the Reds for 1986-87. Again, his contribution was immense. In 54 games that season he scored another 34 goals for Liverpool. After a season at Juventus – 14 goals in 39 games – he was back at Anfield for £2.8 million, and the goals continued. Although hampered by injuries in 1988-89, he came on as a substitute in the FA Cup final against Everton and scored twice in Liverpool's 3-2 extra-time win. He scored 18 times when the League championship was lifted once more in 1989-90.

When he left for Leeds United in 1996, he had scored a record 346 goals in 660 appearances for Liverpool. Shortly after signing for the Reds, Rush had made his full international debut, and his 28 goals in 73 games for Wales was a record until Gareth Bale broke it in 2018. With Liverpool, he gained winners' medals for 5 League championships, 1 European Cup, 3 FA Cups and 5 League Cups. His individual honours include Footballer of the Year, PFA Player of the Year and the European Golden Boot. After Leeds, Rush played for Newcastle United, Sheffield United, Wrexham and Sydney Olympic, and managed Chester. He coached around the world, including working with the strikers at Anfield when Gérard Houllier was manager. He was awarded the MBE and now works as an after-dinner speaker and in the media.

Bruce Grobbelaar

It says as much as anything about the often brilliantly eccentric performances of goalkeeper Bruce Grobbelaar that he bid farewell to his first English club, Crewe Alexandra, by scoring from the penalty spot.

Born in Durban on 6 October 1957, Grobbelaar made a name for himself in South African football before he signed for Vancouver Whitecaps in the NASL. The veteran of 11 months' active service in the Army during the Rhodesian Bush War might have joined West Brom but there were problems in obtaining a work permit. Crewe somehow worked it out, and in December 1979 he joined them on loan. It was Liverpool's chief scout, Tom Saunders, who alerted Anfield, but, his loan spell at an end, Grobbelaar had returned to Vancouver. The Whitecaps manager, former Blackpool and England goalkeeper Tony Waiters, had once been on the coaching staff at Anfield, and in March 1981 Grobbelaar, now a Zimbabwean international, signed for Liverpool for £250,000, as reserve to Ray Clemence.

The surprise transfer of Clemence to Tottenham Hotspur on the eve of the new season gave Grobbelaar his chance. Along with Mark Lawrenson and Craig Johnston, he made his League debut for Liverpool in the 1-0 defeat by Wolves at Molineux in August 1981. He played in every League game that season and was also ever-present for the next 4 seasons, even though his flamboyant style sometimes led to errors that were particularly unwelcome as Liverpool battled to find consistency. When the Reds lost 3-1 to Manchester City at Anfield on Boxing Day, the result propelled John Bond's team to the top of the First Division and left Liverpool mid-table. The *Liverpool Echo* reported that Grobbelaar had come in for much criticism, especially when City were awarded a 74th-minute penalty – he dropped a simple cross and Phil Thompson ended up making a 2-handed save – but reminded readers that his brilliant display at Nottingham Forest in the previous game had led to him being named man of the match: 'His problem at the moment seems to be one of consistency.' But Liverpool were still in Europe and still in the FA Cup – and by the end of the season, after a remarkable turnaround in fortune, they were League champions again.

Between his debut season and when he was given a free transfer to Southampton (he had earlier been out on loan to Stoke City for a couple of months) in August 1994, Grobbelaar made 628 senior appearances for Liverpool. He was missing only when injured, which was rare, and in 1988-89 when he suffered a bout of meningitis that sidelined him for most of the first half of that season.

His antics became a feature of his game, not least in the penalty shootout at the end of the 1984 European Cup final against Roma, when Bruno Conti missed after Grobbelaar started chewing the goal net. Then he wobbled his legs in mock terror as Francesco Graziani stepped up. Graziani also put his penalty over the crossbar and Liverpool won. Grobbelaar also once apprehended a pitch invader and handed him over to police, and there were a few on-field bust-ups with his own teammates as he was never afraid to publicly berate colleagues whom he felt had let him down.

Altogether, Grobbelaar won 6 League championship medals with Liverpool as well as the European Cup, 3 FA Cups and 3 Football League Cups. After Alan Ball signed him for Southampton, Grobbelaar made 40 appearances for the Saints before being on the books of Plymouth Argyle, Oxford United, Sheffield Wednesday, Oldham Athletic, Chesham United, Bury, Lincoln City, Northwich Victoria, Hellenic, and Glasshoughton Welfare, sometimes just for a week or a single game. He later coached in South Africa.

In 1997, at Winchester Crown Court, Grobbelaar was found not guilty of match-fixing. In 2001, the Court of Appeal overturned a High Court verdict against *The Sun* that it had libelled Grobbelaar. In 2002, law lords reinstated the original libel verdict but cut his award from £85,000 to just £1.

Craig Johnston

Few footballers can relate such a story. Craig Johnston was born in South Africa on 8 December 1960, to Australian parents who had met on a boat as they travelled independently around the world. When Johnston was 6 the family moved back to Australia. The boy developed osteomyelitis, a disease that rots the bone. Only the off-chance of a specialist visiting from the USA prevented Johnston from having a leg amputated.

In 1975, he saw Middlesbrough play in New South Wales. He wrote to several clubs, asking for a trial. Boro were the first to reply: they would take a look at it him but he would have to pay his own fare. His mother and father raised the money by moving into a smaller house. The trial match was a disaster. Boro manager Jack Charlton told Johnston that he was the worst footballer he had ever seen and that he should return to Australia (although he did not phrase it as delicately as that). The support of senior players such as Graeme Souness saved him. He earned enough money from cleaning their cars to pay for digs and spent 6 months training on his own and hiding whenever Charlton was around. In April 1977, Charlton resigned, to be replaced by John Neal who gave Johnston, now 17 and catching the eye as a ball-winning midfielder in the youth team, his senior debut, against Everton in the FA Cup in January 1978. One week later, he made his League debut, against Birmingham City.

Three years later, Brian Clough wanted him for Nottingham Forest, while Liverpool, for whom Souness was now playing and putting in a good word for Johnston, were also interested. Johnston telephoned his father for advice. Johnston senior, whose own ambitions to become a professional player had foundered, suggested Liverpool, who were rumoured to be looking to move Jimmy Case out of Anfield.

In April 1981, the previous season's League champions paid Boro £650,000 for the 20 year old who had once been told that he had no future in the game. Case, languishing in the reserves, took a philosophical approach: 'The future looks bleak for me, but I'm not going to rock the boat by asking for a transfer during the season.' After watching Liverpool beat Stoke City 3-0, Johnston mused, 'I'm beginning to wonder where I will fit in.' Terry McDermott, playing on the right side of midfield, where Johnston had prospered with Boro, had scored twice against the Potters.

Fit in he somehow did, his individualistic style bottled to work with the Liverpool way. While Bob Paisley was prepared to use him, Joe Fagan had reservations and in 1984-85, Johnston made only 11 League appearances. It was Kenny Dalglish that gave him a regular game. In 1985-86, Liverpool became only the third team to win the League and FA Cup double in the 20th century. Johnston missed only 4 League games and scored in the 3-1 Wembley win over Everton.

Gradually, though, his form deserted him, and there were family problems back in Australia where his sister lay in a coma following a gassing accident with a faulty heater in a hotel room in Morocco.

His last appearance for Liverpool was as a substitute for John Aldridge in the 1988 FA Cup final, in the shock defeat by Wimbledon. Johnston had made 259 appearances (36 as a substitute) for Liverpool, scoring 39 goals. He had played in 5 League championship-winning seasons, won the FA Cup and 2 League Cups, and the 1984 European Cup. He was capped twice for England under-23s.

Back in Australia, he never forgot Liverpool. He raised £40,000 in his own country for the families of the 96, flew back for the memorial service at Anfield that was held 7 days after the Hillsborough tragedy, and remained for a while to counsel bereaved families.

Craig Johnston has enjoyed a varied life since. He has written a rap record, invented a football boot, created software for hotels to monitor minibar thefts, developed computer models for analysing football statistics, and held exhibitions of his work as a photographic artist.

Ronnie Whelan

Ronnie Whelan came from a football family. His father, Ronnie senior, played for St Patrick's Athletic and Drogheda in the League of Ireland in the 1950s through to the 1970s and was capped twice for the Republic of Ireland. His younger brother, Paul, captained Bohemians to their 1992 FAI Cup win.

Ronnie junior, turned down by Manchester United after a trial, made his debut for League of Ireland club Home Farm on 25 September 1977, his 16th birthday. A few days before his 18th birthday, he was a Liverpool player when Bob Paisley paid £35,000 for a youngster whose midfield industry had caught his eye.

Whelan had to wait for his League debut, but he celebrated it in the Reds' 3-0 win over Stoke City at Anfield on 3 April 1981. In the 27th minute, he took a beautifully weighted pass from Sammy Lee and scored. The following season, Whelan scored 10 goals in 32 games as Liverpool won another League championship. He showed a happy knack of scoring goals in important games, including 2 in the 1982 League Cup final win against Tottenham, and the extra-time winner in the 1983 final against Manchester United. Injured for part of the 1983-84 season, he still played a role in Liverpool winning the treble of League championship, League Cup and European Cup.

In contrast, 1984-85 saw the Reds without a trophy, a campaign that ended with the dreadful night at Heysel. In 1985-86, however, under Kenny Dalglish, it was back to winning ways with the League championship and FA Cup double. Whelan scored 10 goals in 39 League games including a hat-trick when Coventry City were beaten 5-0 at Anfield on 12 April. These were up and down times for Liverpool, though, and 1986-87 was another barren season. The Reds finished runners-up (whisper it gently, to Everton), lost the League Cup final to

Arsenal, 2-1, and were knocked out of the FA Cup by Luton Town, 3-0 in a second replay at Kenilworth Road.

The following season, Whelan was moved from the left of midfield into a central role. John Barnes arrived, there was a new strike partnership of Peter Beardsley and John Aldridge, who between them produced 41 goals, and Liverpool lost only 2 League matches all season to win the title yet again. Because of injury, Whelan played only 28 times and he was also left out of the FA Cup final team that met Wimbledon. Nigel Spackman, who had come in for Whelan earlier in the season, was so far ahead of him in the Wembley reckoning that the Irishman's profile was omitted from the Cup final match programme. Liverpool lost 1-0 to a club that, a decade earlier, had been a non-League outfit.

Whelan was back to skipper Liverpool in 1988-89, when Alan Hansen was injured. Even after Hansen recovered, Dalglish left Whelan with the captaincy and it was he who lifted the FA Cup in May 1989, after Everton were beaten 3-2 after extra-time at Wembley.

In 1989-90, Liverpool were champions again. Whelan missed the last 4 games through injury but was a central presence up until then. There was a remarkable own-goal at Old Trafford in March when he tried a 30-yard chipped back pass that sailed over Bruce Grobbelaar's head and into the net. It was the perfect lob that left the goalkeeper helpless but certainly not speechless.

For the last few seasons of his Liverpool career, Whelan was out injured as often as he played, although his equaliser against Portsmouth in the 1992 FA Cup semi-final forced a replay. Graeme Souness selected him when he could, but at the end of 1993-94, Souness's successor, Roy Evans, let him go to Southend United. Whelan had scored 73 goals in 493 senior games for Liverpool and won 6 League championships, 2 FA Cups, 3 League Cups and the European Cup. He was capped 53 times for the Republic of Ireland. He became player-manager of Southend and coached Panionios in Greece, and Apollon Limassol and Olympiakos Nicosia in Cyprus before a career in the media.

Steve Nicol

Steve Nicol's 70 appearances and 7 goals for Ayr United in the second tier of Scottish football were only a part of his early learning of the game. After he was transferred to Liverpool for £300,000 in October 1981, there followed a season playing for the reserves in the Central League before Bob Paisley gave him his First Division debut, against Birmingham City at St Andrew's in August 1982.

The game, a goalless draw, saw Paisley heap fulsome praise on Phil Neal, who had to play out of position, at centre-half, but he also had a lot to say about new boy Nicol, who played in Neal's usual position of right-back: 'He did well and I was very pleased with him. They put him under a lot of pressure in both halves but he kept his head, and he never panicked. It was a very encouraging start for the young lad.'

Nicol was born in Irvine, Ayrshire, on 11 December 1961 and played for Ayr United Boys' Club before joining the senior outfit in 1979. Having waited a year for his first taste of the big time in England, Nicol did not become a regular first-teamer until 1983-84, when Joe Fagan took over. In 1984-85, Nicol made 29 starts and 2 substitute League appearances as the Reds finished runners-up in the First Division and lost an FA Cup semi-final to Manchester United. Although Nicol had been signed as a full-back, it was in midfield that he found his role in a Liverpool team that was on the crest of wave.

There were hiccups, of course, as there are in any footballer's career. In May 1984, after coming on as a 72nd-minute substitute for Craig Johnston in the European Cup final against Roma, Nicol missed Liverpool's first penalty in the shootout that followed the extra-time stalemate. He put his shot over the crossbar but, fortunately, Neal, Souness, Rush and Kennedy all scored, Roma missed 2 of their spot-kicks, and the trophy was going back on the plane to Merseyside.

There were plenty of highlights for Nicol, however. In September 1987, he scored a hat-trick in a 4-1 win at St James's Park, Newcastle. He had opened that season with the winner at Highbury, a remarkably powerful header from outside the penalty area 2 minutes from the end. It capped a wonderful afternoon for Nicol who had given an all-action display that left the 54,703 crowd – Arsenal's biggest home gate for 6 years – gasping. When Crystal Palace were beaten 9-0 in September 1989, Nicol was the only player to score twice, his goals coming in the 7th and 90th minute.

He was a Liverpool regular until the beginning of the 1994-5 season, when Phil Babb and John Scales were taking over. In January 1995, after 13 years at Anfield, he went to Notts County on a free transfer, signed by their new manager, Howard Kendall.

Nicol had made 468 senior appearances for Liverpool and scored 46 goals in all games, 37 of them coming in 343 League matches. He played in 4 League championship-winning teams, 3 FA Cup-winning sides, and, of course, in the team that won the 1984 European Cup. His 14 Scotland under-21 caps was a record, and he made the first of 27 full international appearances in September 1984, shortly after becoming a first-team regular for the Reds.

At Notts County, he became player-assistant manager, and had his first taste of management after Kendall was sacked, but was unable to save the Magpies from relegation to the Second Division. He left Meadow Lane after playing 32 times in 10 months. He moved to Sheffield Wednesday and was in the Owls team that won 1-0 at Anfield in December 1996. After that he went on loan to West Bromwich Albion, played for Doncaster Rovers and for Boston Bulldogs, a third-tier US club that folded. A long-serving coach of New England Revolution, he was named Major League Soccer's Coach of the Year in 2002. He left Revolution in 2011 and now works for ESPN.

Joe Fagan

Walton-born Joe Fagan was 17 when he signed for Manchester City from Liverpool County Combination Club Earlestown Bohemians in October 1938. The Second World War, in which he served with the Royal Navy, meant that he had to wait until January 1947 to make his Second Division debut but he played in 20 games as City won promotion. After that he was ever-present for 2 seasons, a dependable centre-half who helped City establish themselves back in the top flight. In August 1951, after 158 games and 2 goals for City, he moved to Lancashire Combination club Nelson as player-manager, then played 3 times for Bradford (Park Avenue) in the Third Division North before returning to non-League football with Altrincham and then working as Rochdale's trainer and assistant manager. In May 1958, he joined Liverpool as assistant trainer in succession to Dick Dorsett, who had left some time earlier. When Bill Shankly arrived at Anfield the following year, he was delighted to work with Fagan, whom he had tried to sign from Manchester City when manager of Grimsby Town.

When Shankly resigned in the summer of 1974, Fagan was promoted to assistant manager under Bob Paisley. The logical steps of progression were under way, and when it was Paisley's turn to call it a day, in June 1983, Fagan became Liverpool's sixth manager since the Second World War.

The Reds had just won successive League championships, and in his first season Fagan took them to a hat-trick of titles, something that no club had managed since Arsenal in the 1930s. He bought new players including John Wark from Ipswich Town, Michael Robinson from Brighton and Paul Walsh from Luton Town. Everton were beaten in the League Cup final and then Liverpool won the European Cup for the fourth time, beating Roma on penalties in Rome, all of which meant that Joe Fagan became the first English club manager to win 3 major trophies in a single season. There was, though, the disappointment of

162

Graeme Souness joining Sampdoria, and after sweeping all before them, Liverpool won nothing in 1984-85. Although they eventually finished runners-up to Everton, at one stage the Reds were in 18th place in the First Division. They lost in the semi-finals of the FA Cup, and the third round of the Football League Cup. And then there was the tragic European Cup final in Brussels. Before the game, Fagan, now 64, announced that it would be his last. He told sportswriter Bob Harris:

> There are two reasons why I am giving up the job now. One is that I am too old. The other is that I am too tired. It has been hard work and it needs a younger man. It is a pity someone has let the cat out of the bag before the final but, I suppose, it was almost inevitable as I have been discussing it with chairman John Smith since February.

Of course, like everyone present that dreadful evening, Joe Fagan was extremely upset by what he witnessed as 39 spectators died and another 600 were injured, many seriously, during a confrontation between rival supporters, when fans were crushed against a wall that then collapsed. Fagan had never been one to court publicity and afterwards he kept a very low profile, those closest to him regarding him as a haunted man after the disaster at the Heysel Stadium. He was, though, still a regular visitor to both Anfield and Melwood, ready to offer quiet words of advice to anyone who asked him. And there were plenty who did.

Joe Fagan died from cancer on 30 June 2001, aged 80. He was buried at Anfield Cemetery, close to the scene of his triumphs. It was a great pity that his retirement should have been overshadowed by the events at his last match in charge.

In his biography of Bill Shankly, author Stephen F. Kelly described Fagan as 'a rubber-faced character, as Liverpudlian as the Liver Bird … the psychologist, the genial Scouser, full of Liverpool humour and always grinning.'

Jan Molby

Although blessed with several high-quality midfielders, Liverpool manager Joe Fagan was only too aware that the departure of Graeme Souness to Sampdoria, and the apparent reluctance of Craig Johnston to return from Australia, could leave the Reds vulnerable in the event of injuries in 1984-85. So, Fagan decided to take a closer look at Ajax's 21-year-old Danish international Jan Molby, who arrived at Anfield in August and played his first match in a pre-season friendly against the Dublin club, Home Farm. Suitably impressed, Fagan signed off on the £200,000 transfer and Molby lined up on the opening day of the season as Liverpool began their defence of the League championship against Norwich City at Carrow Road. The game ended 3-3 and Molby might have marked his League debut by snatching the winner but the Canaries' goalkeeper, Peter Hucker, somehow managed to hold on to the Dane's thunderbolt of shot.

Molby kept his place in the First Division side until the home 2-1 defeat by Leicester on Boxing Day, whereupon Fagan dropped him for the next match, at home to Luton Town. His next League appearance was not until 15 May, when he came on as a 27th-minute substitute for Mark Lawrenson against Southampton at The Dell. The Reds and the Saints drew 1-1 and Molby was booked for dissent. He played until the end of the season, coming on once more as a sub, then being substituted before playing the whole 90 minutes in the 1-0 defeat at Goodison on the last day of a campaign that saw Liverpool fail to win a trophy for the first time since 1975.

It was new player-manager Kenny Dalglish who put his faith in Molby, and in 1985-86, as the Reds reclaimed the title, he missed only 3 League matches. He played in the team that beat Everton 3-1 in the 1986 FA Cup final when he had a hand in all Liverpool's goals. He also scored twice, once from the spot, once from open play, when Liverpool beat Manchester United in the fourth round of that season's League Cup.

Molby, who was born in Kolding, Denmark, on 4 July 1963, and played for his local club before moving to Ajax in July 1982, began to assume more responsibility including taking penalties. On 28 September 1985, when Spurs were beaten 4-1 at Anfield, he scored twice from the spot, in the 61st and 67th minute. In November 1986, he scored a hat-trick of penalties against Coventry City in the fourth round of the League Cup. Three days later, he scored another penalty when Coventry visited Anfield for a League game.

In the pre-season of 1987, Molby broke a bone in his foot, which kept him out for most of the season. He returned to the League team only in January 1988, and made just 1 full appearance and a further 6 coming off the bench. It was deputising for the injured Alan Hansen in the centre of defence in 1988-89 that Molby finally regained a regular place. In October that season, however, he was sentenced to 3 months' imprisonment after being found guilty of reckless driving in a 100mph chase by 3 police cars through a built-up area in what his defending counsel described as 'two minutes of madness'. He returned to the side in January, but was injured again and out for the remainder of what had been for him a nightmare season.

In November 1990, he might have gone to Barcelona for £1.5 million but negotiations broke down. In contrast, he later went on loan to both Barnsley and Norwich City before, in February 1996, aged only 32, becoming player-manager of Swansea City. In 292 appearances for Liverpool he scored 61 goals, 42 of them penalties. He won 2 League championship medals (he made only 1 start when the title was won in 1987-88) and 2 FA Cup winners' medals. He was capped 33 times for Denmark and also managed Hull City and Kidderminster Harriers, who he took into the Football League in 2000.

Peter Beardsley

When Glyn Hodges signed for Newcastle United from Wimbledon in July 1987, he told Newcastle's *The Journal*, 'Obviously I'll be disappointed if Peter Beardsley does move because he's probably the best player in Britain at the moment.' Hodges was going to be disappointed. Two weeks later, Beardsley signed for Liverpool for a British record £1.8 million.

The transfer, along with that of John Barnes, had dragged on a bit. The *Liverpool Echo's* Ian Hargraves commented, 'Times have certainly changed since the days of Bill Shankly, when those invited to move to Anfield arrived almost before he had put down the phone.' In Beardsley's case, it was the player wanting a payment from Newcastle in recognition of his 4 years' service and the profit that the Magpies would make on his transfer that had held up the move.

When the signing eventually happened, Beardsley expressed delight at joining 'one of the best clubs in the world'. Liverpool chairman John Smith told a press conference, 'In life, patience is a virtue so Peter was worth waiting for. Not only is he one of the best players in the country, in my book he is the leading player in Europe and the world. Liverpool Football Club can count themselves very fortunate in signing him.'

Yet early in his career Beardsley found that football clubs did not rate him all that highly. Born at Longbenton, Newcastle, on 18 January 1961, he played for Wallsend Boys' Club and was turned down by Newcastle United, Gillingham, Burnley and Cambridge United before Carlisle United took a chance in him. It worked. In 1981-82 he helped them win promotion to the Second Division. Beardsley's decision to move to Vancouver Whitecaps in the NASL was called 'foolish' by Brian Watson, Carlisle's chief scout when Beardsley signed for them. 'The time to go to America is when you're 30, not 20,' he said. In September 1982, however, Beardsley was back in England, signed by Manchester United for £250,000. He played only once for United, in a League Cup match against Bournemouth, before returning to Vancouver from where Newcastle, the club that could once have had him for nothing, paid £150,000 to take him to Gallowgate in September 1983.

Forming a famous partnership with Kevin Keegan and Chris Waddle, he helped Newcastle to promotion to the top flight in 1983-84, won the first of his 59 England caps and played in the 1986 World Cup finals in Mexico before Liverpool signed him. He had scored 61 goals – many of them spectacular strikes – in 162 games for Newcastle, where his pace and superb ball control in tight situations made him a crowd-pleaser.

In 1987-88, Beardsley and Barnes, along with John Aldridge, who had been signed earlier in the year, terrorised opposing defences. Between them they scored 56 of Liverpool's 87 goals – Beardsley scored 15 – as the Reds won the League championship again. It was Beardsley's goal against Spurs at Anfield in April that clinched the title. He played an important role when Liverpool regained the championship in 1989-90, although he missed the last 8 League games of the season because of a knee injury.

The 1990-91 season was, for him, a strange one. He scored a hat-trick against Manchester United in September, and 2 goals at Goodison a week later, but was then out for 6 weeks with an ankle injury. After Souness took over as manager from Dalglish, and spent a record £2.9 million on Dean Saunders from Derby County, Beardsley joined Everton, returning to Newcastle, where Keegan was now manager, in July 1993. He had scored 59 goals in 175 games for Liverpool. He later played for Bolton Wanderers, went on loan to Manchester City, rejoined Keegan at Fulham and played for Hartlepool United before bringing down the curtain on his playing career in Australia when he was 38. He was England caretaker manager Howard Wilkinson's assistant and coached at Newcastle United before, in September 2019, being suspended from all football activity for 32 weeks after an independent FA panel found him guilty of racially abusing Newcastle's young black players.

John Barnes

Will he? Won't he? In June 1987, sportswriters and fans wanted to know if John Barnes would commit to Liverpool. Watford were ready to sell him and the Reds were the only club to have put in a bid. It was now up to the player, who was on his way back to the UK from the Hornets' post-season trip to China. Apparently Barnes, who had come on as England's last hope in the World Cup 12 months earlier, could not understand why no one else wanted him.

In the *Liverpool Echo*, Ian Hargraves reported that Barnes was sitting at home, trying to make up his mind. 'If I can't go abroad, then I'd prefer to remain in London with a club like Arsenal or Spurs,' said a forlorn Barnes. 'I simply cannot believe that they are not interested in signing me. Naturally, I am flattered that a club like Liverpool have made a firm offer, and I could also decide to stay at Watford, though I have not had a chance to talk to the new manager [Dave Bassett] yet.'

Three months earlier, Barnes had been persuaded that he should leave Watford and that bigger clubs would queue up to sign him. A dip in form following the announcement that he wanted away had seen George Graham say that Arsenal were not interested, while David Pleat at Spurs remained tight-lipped. Manchester United declined. There was talk of a move to Italian giants Roma, but when it came to signing John Barnes, it was a 1-horse race.

Even Liverpool officially pulled out of the transfer but, 2 weeks later, Barnes signed, saying that his comments had been taken out of context. He told the *Liverpool Echo*'s Ken Rogers, 'I've built up a tremendous amount of respect for the entire Liverpool set-up. They have always had a tremendous side .... . I believe they are the best club in England, on or off the field. I will do my best for them.'

Kenny Dalglish paid £900,000 for the 23-year-old Jamaican-born forward – he came to England as a 12 year old when his Army officer father was posted to London – who for Watford had scored 83 goals in almost 300 appearances over 6 seasons.

His apparent reluctance to move to Merseyside was soon put behind him. Over the next decade he won 2 League championships with Liverpool as well as 1 FA Cup (he missed the 1992 final because of injury) and 1 Football League Cup, and took his number of full England appearances – he was first capped when he was only 19 – to 79 (48 with Liverpool). His first England goal was a memorable one, against Brazil in the Maracana Stadium in June 1984. It was sensational and brought with it huge expectation.

From his very first season at Anfield, Barnes made a great impact. In that season Liverpool won the League championship, and Barnes scored 15 goals. At the end of it he was voted Footballer of the Year and PFA Player of the Year. In a team of outstanding players, he stood out, on the left, running at defences, the absolute master of the ball at his feet, with a blistering shot. He was an individualist who somehow fitted in with the Liverpool style that was firmly based on great teamwork. With John Aldridge, Peter Beardsley and Barnes up front, and Ray Houghton coming through from midfield, Liverpool were almost unstoppable.

When Liverpool won the League championship again in 1989-90, Barnes scored 22 goals and was again voted Footballer of the Year. There was a frosty relationship with manager Graeme Souness, and at least 1 serious injury, but when he left for Newcastle United on a free transfer in August 1997, he had made 407 appearances for the Reds, scoring 108 goals. Isolated at Newcastle when Ruud Gullit took over, he ended his playing career with Charlton Athletic. He had success managing the Jamaican national team but spells in club management with Celtic and Tranmere both ended badly. John Barnes was awarded the MBE in 1998.

John Aldridge

When John Aldridge signed for Liverpool from Oxford United, for £750,000 in January 1987, he was 28 years old and had probably felt that the chance of him joining the club he had openly supported since boyhood had long gone. Liverpool-born on 18 September 1958, he was working as a tool fitter in a Speke factory and playing as a part-time professional with South Liverpool in the Northern Premier League when Fourth Division Newport County signed him in April 1979. He scored 5 times in his first 6 League games and by the end of the season was top scorer with 14 goals in 38 matches as Newport finished third and were promoted.

In March 1984, Third Division Oxford United paid £78,000 for Aldridge who had scored 80 goals in 194 League and Cup games for Newport, and at the Manor Ground the goals continued to flow – 88 in 127 senior appearances as Oxford went from the Third Division to the First in consecutive seasons. It was the sort of form that attracted bigger clubs. In 1987-88, as successor to Ian Rush, who had finally joined Juventus, Aldridge was Liverpool's leading scorer with 26 goals from 36 First Division games – he scored in every 1 of the first 9 matches – as the Reds won the League championship. Unfortunately, when Liverpool met Wimbledon in the FA Cup final that season, Aldridge's penalty miss – the first by a player in a Wembley FA Cup final – cost the Reds dear as the cherished League and Cup double went with it.

When Rush returned from Italy for the 1988-89 season, Aldridge's response was magnificent. He scored a hat-trick in the opening match, against Charlton Athletic at The Valley, and finished top scorer again, this time with 21 goals from 35 games. In that season's FA Cup final, against Everton, he made amends for his miss from the spot a year earlier by scoring with his first touch after only 4 minutes. Liverpool won 3-2 after extra-time. Aldridge already had a Football League Cup winners' medal from his days with Oxford, and so that completed a nice set of top domestic honours.

At the start of 1989-90 it appeared that Kenny Dalglish now preferred Rush, his old strike partner, to Aldridge, who was now nearing his 31st birthday, and a transfer to Real Sociedad was arranged. Aldridge was on the bench for the home match against Crystal Palace on 12 September 1989. After 67 minutes, Liverpool were winning 5-0 and Dalglish sent on Aldridge to take a penalty. Thus, he marked his final Liverpool appearance with a goal – the Reds went on to win 9-0 – and at the end threw his shirt into a grateful crowd. Aldridge told the *Liverpool Echo*'s Ken Rogers, 'The gaffer asked me if I fancied it. I was prepared to do anything to please the crowd. It was nice to see it fly in … I'm on my way now, but I've enjoyed every single minute of my time at Anfield.'

Aldridge had scored 63 goals in only 104 senior games for Liverpool, won that 1987-88 League championship and the 1989 FA Cup. He was capped 69 times for the Republic of Ireland, 19 of them with Liverpool, and scored 19 goals for the country for which he was qualified to play through his great-grandmother. After Spain, he returned to Merseyside to play for Tranmere Rovers and in his first season at Prenton Park scored a club record 40 goals. When he retired in 1998, aged 39, he had scored 138 goals in 243 League games for them, bringing his overall career total to 408 goals in 753 games in all competitions. As manager, he took Tranmere to the 2000 Football League Cup final where they lost to Leicester City. Six days after Liverpool knocked Tranmere out of the 2001 FA Cup quarter-finals, and with the club destined to drop into the third tier, he resigned after 5 years in the job. He now works on TV and radio and as a newspaper columnist.

Robbie Fowler

Robbie Fowler was not the first Everton supporter whose first professional club was Liverpool, but few, if any, made such an impact at Anfield. Born in Toxteth on 9 April 1975, Fowler was an instinctive goalscorer right from his schooldays, but somehow Everton missed him. He joined the Reds when he left school in the summer of 1991, and signed professional forms on his 17th birthday the following year. In January 1993, after scoring prolifically for the youth and reserve teams, he was named as 1 of the substitutes for an FA Cup third-round replay against Second Division Bolton Wanderers at Burnden Park.

Graeme Souness had included Fowler in the squad simply to give him a taste of what it was like to be around the first team, but when Ian Rush was ruled out with a groin injury there was speculation that the 17-year-old England youth international would make his debut. In fact, Fowler did not get on the pitch that evening – Liverpool lost 2-0 – nor at any time in a season when the Reds finished sixth and made early exits from both domestic cups. But when he did, he made an immediate impact.

He made his first-team debut the following September, scoring in the first leg of a second-round Football League Cup tie at Fulham. A week later, he scored all of Liverpool's goals in their 5-0 win in the second leg. On 30 October 1993, in only his fifth League game, he scored a hat-trick against Southampton at Anfield, and by the end of the season was second only to Ian Rush in Liverpool's scoring chart, with 12 goals from 28 games (Rush had 14 from 42 appearances). Fowler was outright leading scorer in all games with 18 goals, despite being out for several weeks after he broke an ankle against Bristol City in the FA Cup. In 1994-95, Fowler played in every minute of every League game and top-scored with 25 goals, 13 ahead of Rush who missed 6 games. The Reds, with Roy Evans now manager, climbed from eighth in 1993-94 to fourth place. They won the League Cup, beating Bolton 2-1 at Wembley to gain ample revenge over the Trotters.

Robbie Fowler was now one of the most potent strikers in English football. At 4 minutes 33 seconds, his hat-trick against Arsenal on 28 August 1994 is still the fastest in Premier League history. By the following season he was undoubtedly one of the best strikers in Europe.

There were more goals and more medals, but also more injuries, while some on-field antics – such as presenting his backside to Chelsea's Graeme Le Saux whose sexual orientation had been questioned (apparently because he read *The Guardian*), pretending to 'snort a line' in response to Everton fans taunting him as a 'smackhead', and unsubstantiated rumours that he had fallen out with Michael Owen, all got in the way. In November 2001, Gérard Houllier sold Fowler, who had been capped 22 times for England, to Leeds United for £11.75 million. Houllier said that he did not want to sell him but that Fowler wanted to leave. In January 2006, Fowler was back at Anfield. He had spent 14 months at Leeds (he won another 4 England caps there) and 3 years at Manchester City, who paid £6 million for him. But now he was back home, on a free transfer. Reds manager Rafael Benitez said, 'It's a boost to the team and a boost to the supporters. I'm not sure I've ever seen a player so happy to join a club before.' Fowler's final appearance for Liverpool was on the last day of the 2006-07 season. In all, he scored 183 goals in 369 games for the Reds. With them he won 1 FA Cup, 2 Football League Cups (in the 2001 final against Birmingham City he opened the scoring with a 25-yard shot), and 1 UEFA Cup (when he scored in the final against Alavés). He ended his Football League career with Cardiff City and Blackburn Rovers, then played and managed in Thailand and Australia.

Patrik Berger

It was another of those long-running transfer sagas. In July 1996, Liverpool manager Roy Evans had pursued Borussia Dortmund's 22-year-old midfielder Patrik Berger. Berger had spent only a season in the Bundesliga, making 25 appearances, 12 of them from the bench, as Dortmund won the title, but his performances in Euro 1996 had alerted big clubs to the former Sparta Prague player. Liverpool's £3 million bid was on the table for the Czech Republic international who had scored from the penalty spot when the Czechs lost to Germany in the Euro final at Wembley. Eventually, Dortmund accepted a new bid, of £3.25 million, and the player signed in August. All that remained to be sorted out was his work permit.

Some people had reservations. Phil Thompson was one of them. Writing in the *Liverpool Echo*, the former Liverpool star said that he was still 'sitting on the fence a bit' about whether Berger would turn out to be a good buy. Still, said Thompson, it answered supporters' call for a new signing during the summer. He just hoped that the dressing-room banter did not prove too much for a foreign player:

> If his English isn't too good, I would say that his priority
> is that he tries to learn the language as quickly as possible,
> so he is able to communicate on and off the field. This is
> especially important in a place like Liverpool where the
> humour can be very quick.

Berger and his family settled in Southport, where Kenny Dalglish and Alan Hansen were neighbours. He made his League debut as a substitute – 1 of 3 used by Liverpool that day; Jamie Redknapp and Neil Ruddock were the others – in a 2-1 win over Southampton at Anfield on 7 September 1996, and played well enough in his first few games for supporters to warm to him. His second appearance, coming on for Stan Collymore at Filbert Street, saw him score twice as the Reds beat Leicester City 3-0 to go to the top of the table. The following week, Chelsea were hammered 5-1 at Anfield and again Berger scored twice. A fifth goal in only 4 matches came when he scored against MyPa of Finland in the European Cup Winners' Cup. Then the goals dried up: at the end of his first season with Liverpool, Berger had scored 9 times in 34 appearances in all competitions.

The following season, Berger found himself often named as a substitute, although there were still some highlights. In 5 October 1997, when Chelsea lost 4-2 at Anfield, Berger weighed in with a hat-trick. There were also some low moments. In March 1998, Berger refused to be used as a substitute against Bolton Wanderers, after which Evans made it known that he was willing to sell a player whom he felt did not appreciate the value of teamwork. Berger, meanwhile, expressed a desire to join his countryman Karel Poborsky at Benfica, who were managed by Graeme Souness.

It was the appointment of Gérard Houllier as co-manager that changed everything for Berger. Evans's subsequent departure saw Berger gain a regular place until he was carried off during the 4-3 defeat at Leeds in November 2000 after suffering a recurrence of a knee injury. He was flown to the USA where he underwent surgery by leading Colorado-based specialist Richard Steadman.

Berger recovered to play in Liverpool's winning FA Cup and UEFA Cup final teams in 2001. He came on as a 78th-minute substitute against Alavés, and he supplied the pass from which Michael Owen scored the winner against Arsenal at the Millennium Stadium.

His final days at Anfield were disrupted by yet more injuries. When he joined Portsmouth on a free transfer in 2003 he had scored 35 goals in 195 appearances for Liverpool. After Portsmouth, he played for Aston Villa, went on loan to Stoke, and ended his career back at Sparta Prague. He won 42 caps and scored 18 goals for Czechoslovakia and the Czech Republic. After retiring, Berger eschewed coaching work and instead became an ambassador for Liverpool.

Michael Owen

Sportswriter Henry Winter was in no doubt. After scoring on his League debut, at Wimbledon on 6 May 1997, 17-year-old Michael Owen 'is clearly destined for a healthy career'. Liverpool lost 2-1 that evening, but Owen's goal provided a bright spot for the Reds. In *The Daily Telegraph*, Winter described it: 'With 16 minutes remaining, the teenager scored, racing on to Bjornebye's pass before calming sliding the ball past Neil Sullivan.'

It was the first of 158 goals that Owen would score in 297 appearances for Liverpool. The son of Terry Owen, a forward who made 332 League appearances for 6 clubs including Everton (for whom he played twice), Michael Owen was born in Chester on 14 December 1979. Liverpool spotted his schoolboy talent and he was soon given his first-team chance and took it in style. Manchester United, Chelsea and Arsenal had also been interested in signing such a prodigious schoolboy talent who had attended the FA's School of Excellence at Lilleshall at 14, but Owen fell in love with the Liverpool set-up and there was no other club to which he was going to commit.

In his first full season of 1997-98, he was the Reds' leading League scorer with 18 goals from 36 games. He repeated the feat in 1998-99, this time from only 30 appearances. And then he did it again and again, the club's leading scorer in every season up to and including 2003-04. In 2000-01, when Liverpool lifted a treble of FA Cup, Football League Cup and UEFA Cup, Owen received the Ballon d'Or, the annual award given by *France Football* magazine and awarded to the player deemed to have performed the best over the previous year as voted, at the time, by football journalists, although since 2007 coaches and captains of national teams can also vote.

Right from his debut, Owen amazed experienced coaches and managers with a skill and poise that belied his years. He was 17 years and 143 days old when he played against Wimbledon, making him the youngest goalscorer in the club's history. It took him only 6 minutes to score his first European goal, against Celtic at Parkhead on 16 September 1997, and the following year his reported £10,000 a week – his new contract was for 5 years and so worth £2.6 million – made him the highest-paid teenager in British football. On 11 February 1998, he made his full England debut against Chile at Wembley. He was 18 years and 59 days old, the youngest England player of the 20th century. It was the first of 89 caps, during which Owen scored 40 goals. Sixty of those caps came when he was a Liverpool player.

When he was transferred to Real Madrid in August 2004, for £8 million plus Antonio Núñez, Owen could look back on a Liverpool career in which he had won a UEFA Cup, an FA Cup and 2 Football League Cups. Compared to many Liverpool players of the past, it was not the richest haul of medals – there was no League championship – but he played at a time when the Reds were experiencing a comparatively barren time, which makes his goalscoring record even more remarkable.

For Real Madrid, he scored 13 times in 36 La Liga appearances before signing for Newcastle United in August 2005, for £16.8 million. Alas, his time at St James's Park was plagued by injuries and after he was injured during the 2006 World Cup finals, Newcastle received £10 million in compensation. He allowed his contract to run out as Newcastle were relegated from the Premier League in 2009, and – controversially for Liverpool fans – joined Manchester United as a free agent in July that year. In September 2012, he went to Stoke City, announcing his retirement at the end of the season. It was the finale of a career that had seen Owen score 222 goals in 482 senior games in England and Spain. He felt that had he been better looked after by a succession of managers, that record could have been even greater.

Gérard Houllier

In the summer of 1998, Gérard Houllier was one of the most wanted men in football. The 51-year-old former manager of the French national team and current technical director of the French Football Federation was attracting interest from Liverpool, Everton, Celtic, Sheffield Wednesday and Norwich City as well as unnamed French clubs.

Celtic looked to be the overwhelming favourites but, on 16 July, it was announced that he was going to Anfield as joint team manager alongside Roy Evans. Liverpool's vice-chairman, Peter Robinson, a friend of Houllier since the Frenchman was a schoolteacher on Merseyside in 1969-70, stressed that Evans had been fully involved in the decision, which followed the retirement of chief coach Ronnie Moran after 49 years at Anfield.

Houllier's name had connected with Liverpool for over a year, but the club's refusal to sack Evans made it no more than a whisper. The *Liverpool Echo*'s John Parrott wondered how the arrangement would work but felt it a bold move and unfair to condemn it even before the pair had taken their first training session together. By November, however, Evans – 'the last of the Shankly Boys' – was gone, and Houllier became the first Liverpool manager since Bill Shankly's appointment in 1959 to have no previous connection with the club. Continuity was maintained, however, when Phil Thompson was named as Houllier's assistant.

Thus far, the 1998-99 season had been a disappointment. Under the Houllier-Evans regime, Liverpool had been knocked out of both the UEFA Cup and the Football League Cup and stood 11th in the Premier League. The announcement was made at an emotional press conference at which chairman David Moores said that it was a sad day. It had been agreed by mutual consent that Evans, together with coach Doug Livermore, were leaving. 'I could talk for hours about Roy and my respect for him,' said Moores. Evans said, 'I have felt over the past

3 or 4 weeks that things have not been working out ... . I dispute my record is one of failure, though. At any other club it would be a success. But not at Liverpool.'

Houllier now embarked on what he described as a 5-year rebuilding programme. Liverpool finished the season in seventh place and were knocked out of the FA Cup in the fourth round at Old Trafford. There was a slight improvement in 1999-2000, to fourth place although there were still early exits from both domestic cups. But then in 2000-01, the Reds won a unique treble of FA Cup, Football League Cup and UEFA Cup, and finished third in the Premier League to qualify for the European Champions League. This was the Liverpool of Owen, Gerrard, McAllister, Fowler, Berger, Hyypiä, Westerveld, Babbel, Henchoz, Carragher, Hamann and Barmby. In August, the Reds also won the UEFA Super Cup against Bayern Munich and the FA Charity Shield against Manchester United.

The year 2001 had seen a remarkable turnaround. In October, however, Houllier fell ill during Liverpool's match against Leeds United at Anfield, and was taken to hospital where he underwent emergency surgery for a hitherto undiscovered heart condition. Phil Thompson took over the role, Houllier returning to work 5 months later, and between them they guided Liverpool to runners-up, the Reds' best finish in the Premier League to that point. However, despite big signings, Liverpool failed to qualify again for the Champions League. The 2003 League Cup was the only other trophy they won under Houllier, who was criticised for some of his buys, and also for playing unattractive football. In May 2004, he left Anfield, the biggest casualty of a boardroom power struggle. He would not be allowed to fulfil his ambitions for Liverpool, but the fact remained that the club had fallen well behind the likes of Arsenal, Chelsea and Manchester United.

Houllier later took Olympique Marseille to 2 Ligue 1 titles, managed Aston Villa and worked for the French Football Federation before becoming head of global football for Red Bull. He was awarded the OBE for service to British football and the Order of Légion d'Honneur for services to French football.

Steven Gerrard

The *Boys' Own Comic* would hardly have dared invent him. Roy of the Rovers would have been completely overshadowed by him. Steven Gerrard was a remarkable footballer, a skilful, fast, hard-tackling, goalscoring midfielder who achieved some remarkable feats, many of them as he led the team, for he was one of the most inspirational captains the game has ever seen.

Take Liverpool's Champions League match against Olympiacos at Anfield in December 2004. With 4 minutes left on the referee's watch, the Reds are heading out of the competition. Then Gerrard unleashes a 20-yard shot and his team are through to the knockout stage. Not only that, it was arguably the goal that kept him at Anfield. There was talk of the disillusioned Gerrard moving to Chelsea where there appeared to be a greater chance of European glory. After his goal against the Greeks, *The Guardian*'s Kevin McCarra said of him: 'It was as if he had resolved personally to deliver the level of achievement at Liverpool that will make him content to stay.'

Five months later, Liverpool faced AC Milan in Istanbul, in their sixth European Cup/Champions League final, but their first for 20 years. At half-time, they trailed 3-0 but in the second half, a sensational 6-minute spell saw them level the scores. The goal that set them on the road to the most astonishing comeback was scored by Gerrard, their captain, in the 54th minute, a header from a John Arne Riise cross. Liverpool scored again through Vladimir Šmicer, and although Xabi Alonso saw his penalty – awarded after Gerrard was brought down – saved, he equalised from the rebound and the Reds went on to win a penalty shootout 3-2.

One year later, Gerrard's goal in the dying seconds of the FA Cup final against West Ham United forced extra-time, after which Liverpool won another penalty shootout. The player born in Liverpool on 30 May 1980 had become the talismanic figure of the club he joined at the age of 8 and for whom he made his first-team debut under Gérard Houllier in November 1998 – after Jamie Redknapp was injured – and who truly blossomed under Rafael Benitez's management.

There are so many more memorable moments in the Gerrard-Liverpool story: his spectacular 30-yard goal against Manchester United in March 2001 that set Liverpool up for a 2-0 win, their first success over United for more than 5 years; his 2 goals in the 4-0 win over Real Madrid in March 2009, on his 100th appearance against European opposition; all the goals – on his 400th League appearance – in a 3-0 win over Everton in March 2012, the first Merseyside derby hat-trick since 1982. We could go on … and on. There was the hat-trick inside 18 second-half minutes against Luton Town in the FA Cup in January 2008 in a match that marked Jamie Carragher's 500th appearance for Liverpool. It also brought some relief for Benitez after the club's American owners admitted talking to Jürgen Klinsmann about replacing him.

Gerrard made his full England debut against Ukraine in May 2000. His 114th and final international appearance was 14 years later; only 8 other players have won a century of England caps. He captained England on 38 occasions and scored 21 goals for his country.

With Liverpool, Gerrard won the Champions League in 2005, the UEFA Cup in 2001, the FA Cup in 2001 and 2006 and the Football League Cup in 2001, 2003 and 2012. He was voted Footballer of the Year in 2009, the PFA Player of the Year in 2006, and the PFA Young Player of the Year in 2001.

He made his final appearances for the Reds on 24 May 2015, at Stoke. It brought to an end a club career in which he made 710 appearances (504 of them League matches) and scored 186 goals (120 in the League). He played for LA Galaxy in Major League Soccer and was briefly Liverpool's youth manager before becoming manager of Rangers. He was awarded the MBE in the 2007 Birthday Honours List.

Dietmar Hamann

Dietmar Hamann had a short-lived debut for Liverpool. He made his first appearance on the opening day of the 1999-2000 season, at Hillsborough on the same day that other Gérard Houllier signings – Sami Hyypiä, Titi Camara, Vladimir Šmicer, Sander Westerveld and Erik Meijer – were introduced. After 26 minutes, Hamann hobbled off the pitch suffering from ruptured ankle ligaments. It was a sorry sight. Less than 3 weeks earlier, Houllier had spent £8 million of Liverpool's money to sign the German international midfielder from Newcastle United.

Hamann, though, proved to be a quick healer. Forecasts that he would be out until Christmas proved pessimistic. Six matches later, he returned to action, although it would be November before he looked back to full fitness, after which he missed only 1 Premier League game in an overall disappointing season for the Reds.

Hamann, born in Waldsassen in Bavaria, on 27 August 1973, began his career with FC Wacker München before joining Bayern Munich as a 16 year old. With Bayern, he won the Bundesliga title twice and the UEFA Cup before Kenny Dalglish signed him for Newcastle, for £5.5 million after Hamann had starred for Germany in the 1998 World Cup. The following season, Houllier brought him to Anfield.

Hamann's season at St James's Park had, like his early days with Liverpool, got off to a disappointing beginning when he was injured after only 3 matches. Like his Liverpool start, however, he soon overcame the problem and ended with 28 League appearances and 4 goals, enough to persuade Houllier to add Hamann's name to the Reds' summer shopping list.

Not all of Houllier's purchases were outstanding successes, but Hamann proved his worth. In his 7 years at Anfield he was a big influence. In his second season with the Reds he shared in the unique treble of UEFA Cup, FA Cup and League Cup as they also finished third to qualify for Champions League football. In the 2003 League Cup win over Manchester United, he laid on Michael Owen's 86th-minute goal. In the incredible Champions League final comeback in Istanbul in 2005, he broke a toe after coming on for Steve Finnan at half-time. When the game went to penalties, he shrugged off the injury to score Liverpool's first spot-kick. Earlier in the competition, against Bayer Leverkusen, he had scored an 89th-minute free-kick as Liverpool won 3-1.

Hamann also had a happy knack of coming on as substitute with great success. In the 2006 FA Cup final, Liverpool were losing 3-2 to West Ham United when he came off the bench. Steven Gerrard levelled the scores to take the match to extra-time, at the end of which it was still stalemate. Once again, Hamann scored the first in the penalty shootout that followed and which Liverpool won.

That season had not been an overall success for Hamann, however. He was now 32 and started only 13 League games as Momo Sissoko took preference. Rafael Benitez was fair: he told Hamann that he was unlikely to feature much in 2006-07. In the close season, he signed for Bolton Wanderers, then quickly regretted his decision to join the Trotters. Manchester City sounded the better option and after only 24 hours as a Bolton player, he moved to City who agreed that Bolton should receive £400,000 for the player they had for only a day.

Hamann spent 3 seasons with City, taking his overall tally of club appearances in England and Germany to over 500 by the time his contract expired in July 2009. After a year out of the game he became player-coach at Milton Keynes Dons, then joined Leicester City as first-team coach in February 2011. Five months later he was manager of Stockport County who had been relegated to the Conference, but he left there in November 2011 after a proposed takeover of the club failed to happen. There followed a new career in the media, both on television and in print. Hamann, who won 59 caps (42 while with Liverpool) made 283 appearances and scored 11 goals for the Reds.

Rafael Benitez

Some good managers were never more than average players. Rafael Benitez is one. His career was spent in the lower divisions of Spanish football, with Linares, AD Parla and Castilla, albeit they were effectively Real's reserve team. At the age of 26, he joined Real's coaching staff where he was eventually promoted to assistant manager of the first team before, in 1995, seeking the top job, first at Real Valladolid and then to Osasuna. It was with Extremadura that he prospered, taking them back to the top flight in 1997. They were soon relegated, though, and he left. In 2000, he was back in La Liga with Tenerife but he really came to wider notice when he won La Liga with Valencia in 2001-02. More success followed – another La Liga title and the UEFA Cup – before, in June 2004, he replaced Gérard Houllier at Liverpool.

One of 44-year-old Benitez's first tasks was to persuade the unsettled Steven Gerrard to stay. In that he succeeded, but he could not keep Michael Owen at the club; the lure of Real Madrid proved too much for Owen to agree to a contract extension. Then Benitez began to offload players for whom he could not see a future with Liverpool. He liked players from his homeland and Luis Garcia and Xabi Alonso were the first to join.

His first domestic season was a huge disappointment. Liverpool finished fifth, 3 points behind Everton, to whom they lost 1-0 at Goodison Park but beat 2-1 at Anfield. That summed up Liverpool's problem in 2004-05: they lost only 3 of their 19 home games but 11 of those on their travels. They went out of the FA Cup in the third round, at Burnley, and although they reached the Football League Cup final, Chelsea beat them 3-1 at the Millennium Stadium in Cardiff.

All that was forgotten on a May evening in Istanbul. Liverpool's road to the Atatürk Olympic Stadium had been a long and often difficult journey. It had begun back in August, in the third qualifying round in

Austria where, thanks to goals from Gerrard, Liverpool won 2-0 against AK Graz before losing the second leg 1-0 at Anfield. Then followed the group stage where Liverpool finished second behind Monaco, with Olympiacos behind them on the same number of points. Bayer Leverkusen, Juventus and Chelsea were beaten in the knockout stages, and then there was that glorious comeback against AC Milan. For some time afterwards at least, all else was forgiven if not forgotten.

A gripping FA Cup final victory against West Ham 12 months later was followed by another Champions League final in 2007, again with AC Milan the opposition. This time, however, there was to be no sensational fightback. When Dirk Kuyt scored for Liverpool in the 89th minute, Milan were already 2-0 ahead. There was no time for more heroics.

New owners of the club, in the shape of the Americans George Gillett and Tom Hicks were now on the scene, and although Benitez was able to sign Fernando Torres, Yossi Benayoun and Javier Mascherano, Liverpool's results pleased no one at Anfield as the headlines now seemed to be more about off-field discord than about anything that was happening on the pitch. At one stage the owners seemed quite happy to let it be known that they would prefer Jürgen Klinsmann to take over.

Liverpool's status as one of the clubs that always competed in the Champions League was eroding, and a semi-final place in the new Europa League was little compensation. Although in March 2009, Benitez signed a new 5-year contract, in June 2010 he bid a dignified farewell to Liverpool. What had appeared to be the beginning of a new era for the club had not materialised following the fractured relationship between the new owners and the manager.

Benitez had a short spell as manager of AC Milan, won the 2013 Europa League as interim manager of Chelsea, and managed Napoli, Real Madrid and, until June 2019, Newcastle United whom he saw relegated and promoted immediately.

Jamie Carragher

January 1997 was an interesting month for Jamie Carragher. He made his Liverpool debut in a League Cup fifth-round defeat at Middlesbrough, when he came on as a 74th-minute substitute for Rob Jones. His Premier League debut came 3 days later, again as a substitute, this time replacing Neil Ruddock in a goalless draw at Anfield. A week after that he scored his first Liverpool goal, a 50th-minute header from a corner that set the Reds on the way to a 3-0 win over Aston Villa at Anfield. The same month he was named Liverpool's Young Player of the Year – and, just to round everything off, before January was out he celebrated his 19th birthday.

After Carragher's League debut, writing in the *Liverpool Echo* Philip McNulty said, 'Jamie Carragher passed with a purpose and was a willing participant in a couple of bone-shaking challenges. Just put his name down alongside Michael Owen and David Thompson as a star of the future.' Owen's Liverpool career is the stuff of legend. Thompson did not fare so well with Liverpool, making only 48 League appearances.

Jamie Carragher was only just beginning and it is doubtful that anyone could have foreseen the career he would have at Anfield. An Everton supporter born in Bootle on 28 January 1978, he joined Liverpool when he was still at school. Switched from up front to midfield, he helped Liverpool win the 1996 FA Youth Cup final against West Ham. Roy Evans had nurtured the former pupil of the FA's School of Excellence, but it was Gérard Houllier who had the undoubted pleasure of bringing him on in the first team. Once established, only a broken leg, suffered at Ewood Park in September 2003, kept Carragher out for long.

Carragher has never been short of an opinion. After Liverpool lost 1-0 at home to Manchester United in March 2007, a result which left them 19 points behind the Premiership leaders, he was asked what Liverpool required to close the gap. He replied, 'Better players all over the pitch,' before adding, wryly, 'except at centre-half'. After this latest defeat to United, who were down to 10 men when Paul Scholes was sent off, *The Daily Telegraph*'s Tom Rich wrote, 'Wayne Rooney underwent a scan after a fierce tackle from Jamie Carragher, who played with a bloody-minded brilliance and still finished a loser.'

The same month, Rafael Benitez said of Carragher:

> For me, Jamie is one of the best defenders in Europe. He is always focused on the game, always trying to learn... . It is the same every training session, always working hard, always trying to improve ... . He's a strong character, always shouting and talking to the others ... his discipline and organisation is vital.

In February 2013, Carragher announced that he would retire at the end of that season. He marked his final appearance, an emotional affair against QPR, by captaining the team in the absence of the injured Steven Gerrard. He had scored on his first full appearance for Liverpool back in 1997, and he almost scored in his final game, his stunning long-range effort rebounding off a post before he was replaced, late on, to a standing ovation. Liverpool manager Brendan Rodgers said:

> Jamie's ambition was always when he left Liverpool to go out on top and you see in the guy today he did that ... he's going out as a top, top player ... he's been absolutely phenomenal for me in my time here ... today his organisational skills, his quality, his leadership were first class.

Carragher had made 737 appearances for Liverpool, scored 5 goals, and won 38 full England caps. He had a winners' medal from the epic Champions League final in 2005, 2 FA Cup medals, 3 Football League Cup medals and a UEFA Cup medal. Only Ian Callaghan stands ahead of him in Liverpool's all-time appearance list.

Today, he is still a famous presence in football, as an analyst for Sky Sports. His charity, the 23 Foundation, supports sick, disabled and disadvantaged children on Merseyside.

Xabi Alonso

Xabi Alonso arrived at Anfield as part of a new beginning – a new manager in Rafael Benitez and new players including Alonso's fellow Spaniard Luis Garcia, who came from Atlético Madrid for £6 million. Alonso arrived at the same time, in August 2004, for £10.7 million from Real Sociedad after a proposed transfer to Real Madrid did not materialise. There was a stuttering start to the season for Liverpool. Alonso made his debut in the third Premier League game, a 1-0 defeat by Bolton Wanderers at the Reebok. It came only days after the Reds had suffered a 1-0 defeat at home to Graz in the third qualifying round of the Champions League, albeit their 2-0 win in the first leg in Austria meant that they went through on aggregate.

The match at Bolton was a double disappointment for the debuting Spaniards. Luis Garcia had a good goal incorrectly ruled offside, and Bolton's midfield, marshalled by the experienced Gary Speed and Ivan Campo, overran the Reds and forced Alonso and Steven Gerrard to the edges of the action. 'We used our brains today,' said Bolton manager Sam Allardyce, 'We slowed it down.'

Benitez could have countered with the fact that Liverpool were hampered by injuries to Harry Kewell and Florent Sinama-Pongolle, and with Djibril Cissé left on the bench, only Milan Baroš was a recognised striker in an unfamiliar starting 11. Instead the Reds' manager pointed out that 'it will take some time for the Spanish players to learn about the physical side in this country.'

Despite Liverpool's indifferent start, Alonso soon had supporters on his side. The 22-year-old Spanish international midfielder seemed to be made for the Liverpool style. All that season, though, Liverpool struggled to get into the Champions League qualifying places, and their cause was hampered when Alonso suffered a broken ankle against Chelsea at Anfield on New Year's Day 2005, an injury that kept him out of the team for 3 months. The tackle by Frank Lampard earned the Chelsea man a yellow card from referee Mike Riley, who denied Liverpool 2 penalties. Alonso recovered in time to play in the Champions League quarter-final second-leg game against Juventus, and at the end of the season he had marked his first in English football with a Champions League winners' medal after the heroics in Istanbul.

He scored some spectacular goals. There was the 65-yarder in the 5-3 FA Cup third-round win at Luton in January 2006, and a goal from a similar distance against Newcastle United at Anfield in September that year. Newcastle's defenders could only watch as their goalkeeper, Steve Harper, stumbled and the ball drifted over his head into an unguarded net for Alonso's first goal since he scored from his own half at Kenilworth Road.

In May 2007, there was another Champions League final against AC Milan, this time in Athens. Like the rest of that season – and quite unlike the events of 2 years earlier – it ended in disappointment. Alonso was now struggling but Benitez kept faith with him and he made 29 starts in the League. In 2007-08, however, he played only 27 times out of a possible 59 matches, even though he scored twice when newly promoted Derby County – on their way to being the first Premiership club to be relegated before the end of March – were thrashed 6-0 at Anfield in September.

In August 2009, Liverpool sold Alonso to Real Madrid for £30 million, a handsome profit on what they had paid Real Sociedad. For the Reds, he had made 210 appearances, scored 19 goals, and won the Champions League, the FA Cup and the UEFA Super Cup. Leaving Anfield was hardly the end of his winning medals, though. The following year, Alonso was a World Cup winner with Spain. He was also in the teams that won the 2008 and 2012 European Championship finals. With Real he won the Champions League (albeit he was suspended for the final) and La Liga before moving to Bayern Munich where he helped in a hat-trick of Bundesliga titles.

Fernando Torres

When, in July 2007, Liverpool paid Atlético Madrid a club record £20.2 million for Fernando Torres, it was reported that the 23-year-old Spanish international striker had to accept a pay cut. He apparently wanted a 6-year contract worth £31.2 million, but had to settle for £130,000 a week, although that was later revised, according to newspaper reports, to £90,000 a week. Whatever the true figure, it seemed that there was no question of Torres's desire to succeed where his fellow countryman, Fernando Morientes, had failed. After joining Liverpool from Real Madrid in January 2005, Morientes had never come to terms with the Premiership's physical side and after making only 41 appearances he returned to Spain.

In contrast, Torres, who had scored 91 goals in 243 appearances for Atlético and who had been given the number-9 shirt previously worn by Ian Rush and Robbie Fowler, said that he did not think that adapting would be a problem: 'I've seen Premiership games on television, and I know that it's harder to get a free-kick in England than in Spain. And I know that expectations are high and that people will want me to score lots of goals – which I will.'

Torres's talent had been obvious ever since he joined Atlético as an 11 year old in 1995. He was the leading scorer in the 2001 European under-16 championships and scored the winner against France in the final. He helped Atlético to promotion to La Liga as they romped away with the Segunda División title, and in 2002 was leading scorer in the European under-19 championships, scoring both goals in Spain's 2-0 win over Portugal in the final. He made his full international debut in September 2003, against Portugal.

Torres's first League game for Liverpool came on 11 August 2007, when he formed a promising partnership with Dirk Kuyt and Ryan Babel in a 2-1 win at Villa. His first goal, beautifully taken, came a week later, on his home debut in a 1-1 draw at home to Chelsea. Chelsea equalised from a controversial penalty, and referee Rob Styles booked 8 players – 9 if you count the fact that he twice showed Michael Essien a yellow card but did not send him off. Perhaps even Torres was taken aback by the spikey nature of it all.

His promise that he would score goals for Liverpool was not an empty one. He found the back of the net 81 times in 142 games. While with the Reds he also scored 12 of his 38 goals for Spain; 40 of his 110 caps were won as a Liverpool player. Alas, if, with the signing of Torres among others, it was the intention of Liverpool's new owners to show their willingness to pay big money to bring success to Anfield, he won no club honours with the club. Memories of his time there are restricted to individual performances. There was his classy goal in Marseilles in December 2007, which set Liverpool on the way to a 4-0 win to qualify for the Champions League knockout stages. Three days earlier, in the last half hour at Reading, Benitez had taken off Torres, Gerrard and Carragher as the home side led 3-1. Earlier in the season, Torres had scored a hat-trick at Reading in the League Cup. He had not played in the previous 2 League games. Benitez was criticised for leaving him out, but he was involved in 33 of 38 games as Liverpool finished fourth. In the Champions League the winner in the San Siro, and goals against Arsenal and Chelsea stood out.

Torres was the most popular striker at Anfield, but in January 2011, his request for a move was eventually granted with a £50 million transfer to Chelsea, with whom he would win the Champions League and the FA Cup (he was an unused substitute in the final against Liverpool) in 2012. In 2014-15 he went on loan to AC Milan and then returned to Atlético Madrid after a loan spell with his first club. In 2018, now 34, he signed for J1 League club, Sagan Tosu.

Luis Suarez

Liverpool were keeping sportswriters particularly busy as January 2011 ebbed away. Fernando Torres was on his way to fourth-placed Chelsea, who were 9 points ahead of the Reds, and Ajax's 24-year-old Uruguayan striker Luis Suarez was heading for Anfield. Chelsea finally got the player they had first targeted the previous summer, although they had to pay a record-breaking £50 million for him. Thus, Liverpool had doubled their 2007 investment on Torres and the new owners did not have to dig deep to find the £22.8 million for Suarez, who, since his £6.4 million move from Groningen in 2007, had scored 111 goals in 159 games for Ajax.

It was Suarez's performances in the 2010 World Cup finals that brought him both fame and infamy. He scored goals, and he also ended Ghana's dream of a semi-final place when he handled on the goal line. Suarez was sent off but Ghana missed the spot-kick and, ironically, Uruguay won a penalty shootout. Some saw it as an act of selflessness because if his team did make the last 4, he would miss it through suspension. Then there were the biting incidents. In November 2010, Suarez bit PSV's Otman Bakkal on the shoulder and was suspended for 7 matches; in April 2013, playing for Liverpool against Chelsea, he bit Branislav Ivanović and was banned for 10 games; and in the 2014 World Cup he was banned from all football-related activity for 4 months after biting Italy's Giorgio Chiellini. Add to that the 8 matches he missed for Liverpool in his first full season for the Reds, after he was found guilty of racially abusing Manchester City's Patrice Evra, and it is obvious that anyone taking on the brilliant striker also had to be prepared to lose him for periods because of his erratic behaviour.

It seemed worth taking the chance. Liverpool had scored only 31 goals in their first 24 League matches of 2010-11, Torres had long made it clear that he wanted to leave, and Suarez had shown that he could cope with moving, not just from 1 country to another but from 1 continent to another. He was only 19 when Groningen paid Nacional €800,00 to take him from Uruguay to the Netherlands in 2006. Even then he had baggage: when he was 16, he headbutted a referee after being sent off.

Putting all that aside (as difficult as it is to do), Suarez was a success for Liverpool, right from his debut, against Stoke City in February 2011 when, after coming off the bench in the 62nd minute, he took a ball from Dirk Kuyt, went around the Potters' goalkeeper Asmir Begović and rolled the ball into the net, although it was helped to its final destination by Stoke defender Andy Wilkinson and a goalpost. Liverpool supporters were delighted, and so was Suarez. He said, 'Just to be on the field for a few minutes and to manage to score in front of the Kop, it's what dreams are made of.' Dalglish was looking forward to Andy Carroll regaining full fitness and partnering Suarez. Together with Gerrard and Raul Meireles they would, said Dalglish, form a 'frightening' attack.

The picture of Suarez is of a player who could be either brilliant – one thinks of his hat-trick at Norwich in April 2012 (he scored another hat-trick at Carrow Road only 5 months later, and he always seemed to have it in for the Canaries; he scored 4 against them at Anfield in December 2013) – or one that was always falling over and complaining. He scored 82 goals in 133 games for Liverpool, but with them won only the Football League Cup in 2012, although there were many individual awards including Footballer of the Year and PFA Player of the Year in 2014. That summer he was transferred to Barcelona for £65 million. With Barca, he has won the Champions League and 4 La Liga titles and he took his total of Uruguay caps well past 100, 40 of them won while at Liverpool.

Daniel Sturridge

When he signed 23-year-old striker Daniel Sturridge for Liverpool in a £12 million transfer from Chelsea in January 2013, Brendan Rodgers advised caution. He told *The Daily Telegraph*'s Chris Bascombe that although Sturridge had got quality, if he wanted to remain playing at that level then this was probably his last chance. Rodgers said, 'We are bringing in a player who knows that he has to perform as he will be playing with one of the biggest clubs in the world.'

For all that, Rodgers signed Sturridge on a long-term contract. Andy Carroll had gone on a season-long loan to West Ham United, and Fabio Borini was out with a broken foot sustained against Manchester United. Support was needed for Suarez, who was coming under intense pressure due to the Reds' lack of other quality strikers.

Birmingham-born Sturridge who came from a football family – his father, Mike, played a handful of games for Wrexham, and his uncles, Simon and Dean, had good careers with a number of clubs – was with Aston Villa's youth academy and then Coventry City before joining Manchester City when he was 13. City had to pay Coventry compensation. They later sold Sturridge to Chelsea in 2009 and with all the contractual add-ons eventually received over £8 million. Sturridge's move from Stamford Bridge to Anfield was good news for City, who were entitled to 15 per cent of any profit from the player's next move.

Sturridge played down reports that he was going to Liverpool because he had been promised a central striking role. 'I believe that is my best position' he said, 'but I've also played on the wing, and I'd never refuse to play there. Whatever the manager wants me to do, I'll do it.'

Sturridge remained at Anfield for over 6 years, during which time he made 160 appearances, scored 67 goals, and was an unused substitute in the 2019 Champions League final victory over Spurs. He played in losing teams in the 2016 Football League Cup and Europa

League finals. Twenty-two of his 26 full caps for England came while he was a Liverpool player. With Chelsea, he had also won the Champions League (he was an unused substitute in the final) as well as the Premier League and the FA Cup. He was also an unused substitute when Chelsea beat Liverpool in the 2012 final.

The start of his Liverpool career saw him score in each of his first 3 appearances, a feat no Liverpool player had achieved since Ray Kennedy in September 1974, when he found the net in 2 First Division matches and a League Cup game. Sturridge's first Liverpool goal was against Manchester United and he scored his first 10 Premier League goals in fewer games than any Liverpool player before him, although Mo Salah has equalled that record. In his first season Sturridge formed, as Rodgers had hoped, a potent partnership with Suarez, Sturridge's contribution being 11 goals in all competitions after joining the Reds halfway through the season.

The following season, as Suarez completed his 10-game ban for biting Sturridge's former teammate Branislav Ivanović the previous April, Sturridge scored 6 goals in 6 games, and after the Uruguayan returned, the pair went on the rampage once more, Sturridge scoring 21 League goals, which saw him runner-up to Suarez who had 31 to give him the Premier League Golden Boot. At the start of Suarez's ban, Sturridge had scored a hat-trick at Fulham in the season's penultimate match.

Injuries then began to disrupt his progress and although he scored a fine opening goal in the 2016 Europa League final against Sevilla, Sturridge was not always part of new manager Jürgen Klopp's plans, and in 2017-18 he went on loan to West Brom. In August 2019, he joined Turkish club Trabzonspor. The previous month, an independent commission had given him a 6-week ban (4 weeks of it suspended) from football and fined him £75,000 for breaching the game's betting regulations. The FA appealed against what it saw as the leniency of the punishment.

Roberto Firmino

On 29 December 2018, Liverpool fell behind at Anfield in the Premier League for the first time in almost a year – 364 days to be precise – when Ainsley Maitland-Niles gave Arsenal an 11th-minute lead. Three minutes later, the Reds were level, through Roberto Firmino. Two minutes after that, Firmino put them in front. Sadio Mané made it 3-1 just after the half-hour mark, Mo Salah scored from the penalty spot well into added time at the end of the first half, and after 65 minutes, Firmino completed his hat-trick when Salah declined the chance to take another spot-kick, handing the ball to Firmino for what Jürgen Klopp described as 'a Christmas present'. Liverpool 5 Arsenal 1.

Firmino, an attacking midfielder, joined Liverpool from TSG 1899 Hoffenheim in July 2015, for almost £29 million. Manager Brendan Rodgers was certainly in need of another goalscorer. Daniel Sturridge was suffering injuries, Luis Suarez had gone to Barcelona, and Steven Gerrard had also played his last game for Liverpool. For Hoffenheim, Firmino had scored 38 goals in 140 Bundesliga matches after signing for them from Figueirense as a 19 year old. He helped Figueirense return to the Brazilian Série A. Now he exchanged the Bundesliga for the Premier League, although to complete the deal Liverpool's CEO, Ian Ayre, had to fly to Chile where Firmino was playing for Brazil in the 2015 Copa América. Once the competition was over, and after Firmino had completed a medical examination, he was a Liverpool player.

He made his debut on 9 August 2015, as a substitute in a 1-0 win at Stoke. His first start came in the third game of the season, a goalless draw at the Emirates in which he was swapped for Jordon Ibe after 63 minutes. Under Rodgers, Firmino was given a wider role and struggled to find the form that had persuaded Rodgers to buy him. In October, however, Rodgers was gone, his place taken by Jürgen Klopp, who was only too familiar with Firmino because the Brazilian had opposed Klopp's former club, Borussia Dortmund, several times. Klopp said that although Firmino was effective coming in from the wing, he was best when playing as an offensive midfielder, or used as a second striker.

After 3 drawn League games, Liverpool's first win under Klopp was against Bournemouth in the League Cup. Firmino, who was described by Klopp as 'the best player in the Bundesliga' for a spell during the previous season, created the winner for Nathaniel Clyne, a £12.5 million summer signing from Southampton.

It was as if Firmino had been liberated under Klopp's management. Three days after the Bournemouth game, in a 3-1 win at Stamford Bridge, he was given the role of Liverpool's central striker, and on 21 November, playing in the same position, he scored once and laid on 2 more as the Reds steamrollered Manchester City 4-1 at the Etihad. One of the goals came from Firmino's fellow Brazilian, Coutinho, who finished off a glorious reverse pass from his countryman.

In his first season as a Liverpool player, once Klopp arrived Firmino quickly became one of the Reds' key men, although there were a few occasions when he was accused of fading out of games. Nonetheless, he ended the season as Liverpool's top Premier League scorer with 10 goals, and as a centre-forward he continued to score goals over the following seasons, and although in 2018-19 he was not as prolific – he missed a few weeks through injury – his goals still helped Liverpool to win the Champions League and he became the highest scoring Brazilian in Premier League history.

In February 2017, he was fined £20,000 and banned from driving for a year after being found guilty of drink-driving. The offence had taken place shortly after burglars had targeted his home. In January 2018, the Everton defender Mason Holgate accused Firmino of racially abusing him but after a long investigation, including evidence from 2 lipreaders, the FA cleared him.

Jürgen Klopp

On 4 October 2015, Liverpool drew the 225th Merseyside derby. It was the fifth time in the Reds' previous 6 games that they had taken the lead, only to draw 1-1. It left them in 10th place. An hour after the final whistle at Goodison Park it was announced that Brendan Rodgers had been sacked. The following day the former Watford, Reading and Swansea City manager, who had replaced Kenny Dalglish at Anfield in June 2012, released a statement through the League Managers Association, part of which read:

> It has been both an honour and a privilege to manage one of the game's great clubs for the last 3 years ... . Liverpool has a magnificent football heritage and I have nothing but respect and admiration for the history, tradition and values that make the city and the club so exceptional.

In a joint Fenway Sports Group statement, principal owner John W. Henry, chairman Tom Werner and president Mike Gordon said:

> We would like to place on record our sincere thanks to Brendan Rodgers for the significant contribution he has made to the club and express our gratitude for his hard work and commitment. All of us have experienced some wonderful moments with Brendan as manager and we are confident he will enjoy a long career in the game. Although this has been a difficult decision, we believe it provides us with the best opportunity for success on the pitch. Ambition and winning are at the heart of what we want to bring to Liverpool. The search for a new manager is under way and we hope to make an appointment in a decisive and timely manner.

The new man was already lined up. Jürgen Klopp, who, in response to being reminded of José Mourinho's 'Special One' remark, said that he was the 'Normal One'. The 48-year-old German, who after a career as a goalscorer with FSV Mainz 05 in the German second tier then managed them in the Bundesliga in 2004, had taken Borussia Dortmund to the Bundesliga title, the DFB-Pokal (the German Cup) and to runners-up in the 2013 Champions League final against Bayern Munich at Wembley. He left Dortmund at the end of 2014-15.

Speaking about managing Dortmund in a pre-season friendly at Anfield, the man with a diploma in Sports Science from Goethe University of Frankfurt, told his first press conference:

> I am a football romantic. I love the stories, the histories. It was my first time at Anfield and I thought about how it would be. I am a really lucky guy. I am looking forward to the first training with the players. I am relaxed. I had 4 months' holiday and am in my best shape … . It is the intensity of the football, of how the people live football in Liverpool, all the Liverpool fans around the world. It is not a normal club, it is a special club.

His first season saw Liverpool reach the finals of the Europa League and the League Cup, but lose both. In 2016-17, he took the Reds to fourth position. That led to the 2018 Champions League final, although it ended in disappointment in Kiev where Liverpool lost 3-1 to Real Madrid after 2 goals from Gareth Bale finished off the Reds who had drawn level at 1-1. But Liverpool were back in Europe, back in the Champions League, and going forward. Twelve months later, after an unforgettable semi-final second-leg 4-0 win over Barcelona at Anfield, they won the Champions League by beating Tottenham Hotspur 2-0 in the final in Madrid.

Klopp proved to be not only a fine tactician, but also one of the game's best-loved characters with his relentlessly cheerful approach. For Liverpool, he brought in players such as Alisson, van Dijk, Fabinho and Naby Keïta. The Champions League was a wonderful achievement but when, in 2020, he delivered Liverpool's first Premier League title after 30 years of waiting, even Jürgen Klopp was reduced to tears.

Alisson

Roma thought they had slipped up when they sold Mo Salah to Liverpool for an initial fee of £39 million in June 2017. Salah's first season at Anfield was nothing short of sensational. So, a year later, when the Reds went back for goalkeeper Alisson Ramses Becker, the Italian club wanted £90 million for the Brazilian international. Liverpool baulked at the figure. Chelsea looked interested, but they were still in the process of selling the unsettled Thibaut Courtois to Real Madrid. When Roma dropped the price to what they later said was a fee – with eventual add-ons – of £66.8 million but which Liverpool insisted was only £65 million, the deal was complete. £66.8 million or £65 million – either way it was a world record for a goalkeeper, more than doubling the £32 million that Juventus had paid Parma for Gianluigi Buffon a full 17 years earlier (20 days after Alisson's record move, Chelsea paid £71 million for Athletic Bilbao keeper Kepa Arrizabalaga).

As the Alisson transfer rumours circulated, Roberto Negrisolo, the former Roma goalkeeping coach, told *Il Romanista* newspaper:

> This guy is a phenomenon. He is the Number One of Number Ones. He is the Messi of goalkeepers, because he has the same mentality as Messi. He is a goalkeeper who can mark an era ... . I know goalkeepers, that is my business, and I can assure you Alisson can be a guarantee for at least another 10 years. He's already a hero to the fans and Roma need to keep hold of him.

Of course, Roma could not keep him. The 25-year-old Alisson had apparently set his heart on a move to Anfield. He has a fine pedigree. His grandfather played for the Porto Alegre-based Sport Club Internacional in Brazil. That was also Alisson's first professional club, from where he joined Roma in 2016, for £5.6 million. Although he made his Roma debut in a Champions League match in August 2016, initially he was the understudy to Polish international Wojciech Szczęsny, and his Serie A debut was delayed until the opening weekend of the 2017-18 season. When Roma reached the Champions League semi-finals in 2018, Alisson did not concede at the Stadio Olimpico in the competition until Sadio Mané scored a ninth-minute goal for Liverpool in the second leg of the semi-final on 2 May. James Milner put through his own goal before Georginio Wijnaldum beat Alisson to restore Liverpool's lead. Roma went on to win 4-2 but it was the Reds who went through to the final, 7-6 on aggregate.

It was probably his first experience of the atmosphere at Anfield that drew Alisson to Liverpool rather than to Chelsea. He made his debut for the Reds on 12 August 2018, in a 4-0 win over West Ham United. His new fans soon began to appreciate what Negrisolo meant when he suggested that Alisson was more than just a goalkeeper. He was not just a simple shot-stopper. In Serie A, he had also set up attacks with defence-splitting passes, and around his penalty area was as sure-footed as any outfield defender. His decision-making was second to none. Liverpool supporters began to wonder, though. In his first season, there were a few hairy moments such as in September 2018 when he tried to dribble past Leicester City's Kelechi Iheanacho, but lost the ball to the Nigerian striker who gave it to Rachid Ghezzal to score from close range to end Liverpool's 100 per cent clean sheet record that season. The Reds still won, thanks to goals from Mané and Firmino, and afterwards Jürgen Klopp tried to put on a positive spin, saying, 'It needed to happen so that it doesn't happen again.'

Such instances could have threatened Alisson's Liverpool career with a hero-to-zero label, but there were also many outstanding moments, not least against Napoli in a Champions League group game when, in blocking Arkadiusz Milik's stoppage-time shot, Alisson probably saved Liverpool from elimination. Instead he ended the season with a Champions League medal, the UEFA Goalkeeper of the Year award and the Premier League's Golden Gloves after he kept 21 clean sheets.

Virgil Van Dijk

On the first day of 2018, 26-year-old Dutch international Virgil van Dijk completed a £75 million-move from Southampton to Liverpool, becoming the costliest defender the game had ever seen. In a single moment, the £53 million that Manchester United had spent on Tottenham's England full-back Kyle Walker in the summer was eclipsed.

Van Dijk told the waiting press, 'With the history of the club, and everything around it … it's just the perfect match for me and my family.' The son of a Dutch father and a Surinamese mother, van Dijk was born in Breda on 8 July 1991. He began his Eredivisie career with FC Groningen and made his debut in May 2011. When he was 20, he was taken seriously ill with peritonitis and kidney poisoning but recovered and continued to the point where it was plain that, if his career was to progress, then he needed to move to a bigger club. But there was no interest from other Eredivisie clubs, and, in June 2013, it was Celtic who signed him for £2.6 million.

With Celtic, he won the Scottish Premiership in 2013-14 and 2014-15, and the Scottish League Cup in 2014-15. In September 2015, after 76 League games for Celtic, van Dijk joined Southampton on a 5-year contract. The Saints manager, fellow Dutchman Ronald Koeman, paid £13 million to take van Dijk to St Mary's. The following month, van Dijk made his full international debut for the Netherlands, in a 2-1 win over Kazakhstan in a Euro 2016 qualifying match.

Liverpool first showed an interest in 2017. Van Dijk was apparently keen on a move to Merseyside, but the correct protocol had not been followed and the Reds apologised to the Saints for what was technically an illegal approach. That year he suffered injuries, an ankle problem ruling him out of the 2017 League Cup final. It was late September before he was fit to return to the first team. His final appearance for the Saints was in mid-December, and just after

Christmas it was announced that he would at last be free to join Liverpool, once the January transfer window opened.

Van Dijk was unavailable for Liverpool's New Year's Day game at Burnley because his registration would not be completed in time. His debut came in the following Friday's FA Cup third-round tie against Everton at Anfield. It was the perfect start: Van Dijk scored the winner with an 85th-minute header to extend Liverpool's run of derby victories to 16. It really was a little piece of history, the first time that a player had marked his debut by scoring in a Merseyside derby since Bill White scored in the second minute of a 2-2 draw at Anfield 14 September 1901.

Van Dijk continued to prove that he was worth every penny of his record transfer fee. His skill and his organisational ability went a long way to Liverpool reaching the 2018 Champions League final. The 2018-19 season was even better. He missed only 1 Champions League game – through suspension – as Liverpool again went to the final and this time won it and he was voted man of the match. In March 2019, he scored the vital second goal when the Reds beat Bayern Munich 3-1 in the Allianz Arena, his 69th-minute header from James Milner's corner giving Liverpool the lead. Van Dijk displayed all his talents that night, his long pass setting up Sadio Mané for an exquisite opening goal. His passing accuracy was amazing and no one won more aerial battles or made more clearances as Liverpool went into the quarter-finals. It was as if he alone had transformed a hitherto suspect defence into one of the meanest in Europe. At the end of the season he was voted UEFA Men's Player of the Year, adding that to his PFA Player of the Year award after starting every Premier League game and helping to keep 21 clean sheets in 38 matches.

After Chelsea beat Manchester City to confirm Liverpool as runaway Premier League champions in the Covid-19-disrupted 2019-20 season, Van Dijk tweeted, 'At the end of a storm, there's a golden sky. We did it! Dreams do come true.'

Mo Salah

Jürgen Klopp had targeted Mo Salah for some time. Indeed, the Egyptian striker had almost joined the Reds from Basel in 2014, when Brendan Rodgers was at Anfield, but instead he ended up at Chelsea. In June 2017, however, the 25 year old finally arrived on Merseyside, a £34-million signing from Roma. It was short of the club record £35 million that Liverpool had spent on Andy Carroll in 2011 but equalled Sadio Mané's fee when he became Africa's most expensive footballer upon joining the Reds from Southampton in 2016. Klopp had tracked Salah since the player's emergence with Basel where he won the Swiss Super League in 2012-13 and 2013-14. He had, said Klopp, a perfect blend of experience and potential, and amazing pace. He would inject even more fire and threat into Liverpool's attack

Salah's £11 million move to Chelsea had not been a success. He made only 13 Premier League appearances and had gone on loan to Fiorentina and Roma before the latter paid £15 million to take him on permanently in the summer of 2016. On Merseyside, he told the press that he was a better player than when he went to Stamford Bridge: 'I was only a kid then, 20 or 21 years old. I was a different person. The experience of being with 3 big clubs has changed me. Everything is different now.'

Salah arrived at Basel from Al Mokawloon Al Arab Sporting Club in 2012, after the Egyptian FA cancelled the remainder of the country's season following a riot in Port Said where 74 spectators were killed and more than 500 injured after an Egyptian Premier League match. His time in Switzerland was marked by those title wins but also by controversy when it was alleged that he avoided shaking hands with Israeli players of Maccabi Tel Aviv before a Champions League qualifying match. There were other alleged indiscretions after he joined Liverpool, from using a mobile phone while driving to being photographed with a Chechen leader accused of human rights abuse, but nothing could take away from his sensational contribution to the Reds on the pitch, or from his considerable charity work for the benefit of people in his hometown of Nagrig, where he donated money to build a school and a hospital.

In his first season on Merseyside, Salah exceeded all expectations. In 52 appearances, he scored 44 goals. As a Liverpool club record it was second only to Ian Rush's 47 goals in all games in 1983-84. Not surprisingly, such a strike rate won Salah a host of personal honours. He took the Premier League Golden Boot, his 32 League goals being a record for a 38-match season. He was voted Footballer of the Year and PFA Player of the Year.

It was a devastating sight to see him forced to leave the action because of a shoulder injury after a challenge by Real Madrid's Sergio Ramos in the 2018 Champions League final. The Serbian referee, Milorad Mazic, gave no foul. An Egyptian lawyer later opened proceedings against Ramos for jeopardising Salah's chances of playing in his country's first World Cup finals in 28 years. Over half-a-million people signed a petition asking FIFA and UEFA to punish the Spaniard whose challenge had resulted in Salah spraining ligaments in his left shoulder after he hit the ground. Salah did play in the finals, although he missed Egypt's opening game and was clearly less than 100 per cent match fit, even though he scored in the defeat by Saudi Arabia.

Salah's 2018-19 season was surely never going to be as prolific but his 22 Premier League goals still earned him a share of the Premier League Golden Boot alongside Sadio Mané and Arsenal's Pierre Aubameyang, and on 1 June 2019, in Madrid, he scored a second-minute penalty to send Liverpool on their way to a Champions League final victory over Spurs.

Bibliography

Books

Andrews, Gordon, *The Datasport Book of Wartime Football 1939-46*, Gardenia Books, 1989.

Gibson, Alfred, and Pickford, William, *Association Football and the Men Who Made It*, Caxton Publishing Company, 1905.

Kelly, Stephen F., *It's Much More Important Than That: Bill Shankly, The Biography*, Virgin Books, 1997.

Rippon, Anton, *Gas Masks For Goal Posts: Football in Britain During the Second World War*, Sutton, 2005.

Rippon, Anton, *The Story of Liverpool FC*, Moorland, 1980.

Shankly, Bill, *Shankly,* Arthur Baker, 1976.

St John, Ian, *The Saint - My Autobiography: The Man, The Myth, The True Story*, Hodder Paperbacks, 2006.

Various contributors, *The Book of Football,* The Amalgamated Press, 1906.

Ward, Andrew, *Scotland The Team*, Breedon Books, 1987.

Newspapers

Athletic News
Belfast Telegraph
Blackburn Times
Cricket and Football Field
Daily Herald
Daily Mail
Dally Mirror
Daily Record

Bibliography

Daily Telegraph
Derby Daily Telegraph
Derbyshire Times and Chesterfield Herald
(Dundee) Courier
(Dundee) Evening Telegraph
Eastern Evening News
Good Morning
Guardian
Lancashire Evening Post
Liverpool Daily Post
Liverpool Echo
Liverpool Evening Express
(Newcastle) Evening Chronicle
(Newcastle) Journal
Northern Whig
Referee
Scottish Referee
Scotsman
Sheffield Daily Telegraph
Sheffield Independent
Shields Daily News
Staffordshire Sentinel
Sunday Post
Sunderland Daily Echo and Shipping Gazette
Weekly News
Wrexham Leader
Yorkshire Post
Yorkshire Post and Leeds Intelligencier

Website

https://www.lfchistory.net

Index